Literacy and Bilingualism
A Handbook for ALL Teachers

Literacy and Bilingualism
A Handbook for ALL Teachers

María Estela Brisk
Boston College

Margaret M. Harrington
Providence Public Schools

LAWRENCE ERLBAUM ASSOCIATES, PUBLISHERS
2000   Mahwah, New Jersey   London

Lawrence Erlbaum Associates, Inc., Publishers
10 Industrial Avenue
Mahwah, NJ 07430

Cover design by Kathryn Houghtaling Lacey

Library of Congress Cataloging-in-Publication Data

Brisk, María.
Literacy and bilingualism : a handbook for all teachers / by María
Estela Brisk and Margaret M. Harrington.
    p. cm.
Includes bibliographical references and index.
ISBN 0-8058-3165-7 (pbk : alk. paper)
1. Education, Bilingual—United States. 2. Literacy—United States.
3. English language—Study and teaching—United States—Foreign
speakers. 4. Second language acquisition. I. Harrington, Margaret
M. II. Title.
LC3731.B684 2000
370.117'5'0973—dc21

                                                    99-31664
                                                    CIP

Books published by Lawrence Erlbaum Associates are printed on acid-
free paper, and their bindings are chosen for strength and durability.

Printed in the United States of America
10 9 8 7 6 5 4 3 2 1

Contents

Preface

GOALS AND APPROACHES

The rise of immigrant students in the United States and, indeed, in most countries, along with the concern for foreign language education throughout the world, requires appropriate tools for teaching literacy. The demands of modern society require high proficiency in literacy. Research and practice have advanced understanding of the reading and writing process. Numerous exciting approaches for teaching reading and writing have emerged from such work. Careful research has proven their effectiveness.

Most of this research has been done with English-speaking students learning to read and write in English as their native language. There are, however, numerous classroom situations where students learn to read and write in a second language. There are students who are native speakers of other languages in more than 50% of the classrooms in the United States where the instruction is in English. For the deaf, English is a second language. Some schools promote English as a second language (ESL) programs where literacy is taught in English. With the advent of bilingual education, literacy is introduced in the students' native languages. English-speaking students learn to read and write in a second language in foreign language classrooms or in bilingual education programs.

We wrote this handbook to apply proven techniques, derived from bilingual–bicultural classrooms, to teaching literacy in the 21st century. Complete and straightforward instructions are accompanied by accounts of teachers experimenting with a variety of approaches[1] to enliven instruction in reading and writing native as well as second languages.

---

[1]We chose the word *approaches* or "the method used or steps taken in setting about a task" (Random House dictionary) rather than *methods* or *strategies*. Approaches better defines the range from very detailed to broader procedures for teaching literacy illustrated in this book.

"The pendulum of approaches to literacy instruction continues to swing as educators debate the merits of skill-based and meaning-based approaches."[2] Those presented in this handbook do not embrace any of these extreme beliefs.[3] Literacy uses need to make sense in order for students to acquire and develop them. In turn, students need skills to make use of literacy. Literacy programs "should be designed to provide optimal support for cognitive, language, and social development, within this broad focus, however, ample attention should be paid to skills that are known to predict future reading achievement."[4]

These approaches share a number of characteristics that help motivate students of varying language abilities to develop literacy. They:

- Encourage students' creativity.
- Tap into students' knowledge as the basis for learning.
- Allow for students to regulate the degree of difficulty.
- Encourage functional uses of languages.
- Reinforce all language skills (listening, speaking, reading, and writing).
- Include engaging activities.
- Encourage student interaction and active participation.
- Practice skills in meaningful contexts.

All approaches recommended in this handbook encourage the integration of all language skills in teaching literacy. However, some emphasize writing, others emphasize reading, yet others work on all language skills, including oral proficiency.[5]

These literacy approaches can be effectively used in classrooms where literacy instruction takes place in a second language. But teachers must modify and adapt these approaches by incorporating students' language and culture and taking into consideration factors affecting bilingual–bicultural individuals. Thus, this handbook analyzes first the characteristics of bilingual–bicultural students and then explains reading and writing acquisition and development for such students.

FIELD-TESTED APPROACHES

The approaches presented in this handbook have been modified and tested with bilingual populations of different ages and language backgrounds in bilingual,

---

[2] Perez (1998, p. 261).

[3] See Gee (1992) for a discussion on the circularity of this debate.

[4] Snow, Burns, and Griffin (1998, p. 9).

[5] Speaking or signing a story, explaining an event, or discussing a topic are part of students' literacy knowledge. This concept is particularly important for teaching the deaf, whose natural language, American Sign Language (ASL), is not written. For more information on teaching deaf students see Paul (1998).

ESL, mainstream, special education, and deaf education classes. Even teachers in special subject classes have tried them. Pauline, a middle school music teacher, used process writing to have her students learn and write about modern American composers. Half of her 40 students were Chinese bilinguals with varying ability in English. These approaches have also been tested in foreign language classrooms in the United States and abroad.

The students ranged from preschool through high school. The students' languages included English, Spanish, Portuguese, Haitian Creole, Hebrew, Cape Verde Creole, Chinese, Greek, French, Japanese, Arabic, Russian, Khmer, Korean, and others.

In all of these languages, as well as in all of these contexts, the authors related linguistic-based strategies to sound educational principles. Stepping back from what they and the numerous teachers they have prepared have learned about how to motivate students to acquire literacy in either their native or second languages, they describe techniques that are readily available to teachers entrusted to develop the basic educational skill, literacy.

This handbook makes the most successful approaches available to other university classes, to professionals leading workshops, and to teachers themselves who wish to experiment on their own. Each approach has been utilized in a variety of settings. At first, teachers were skeptical about whether specific approaches would work in their classrooms. Some secondary school teachers initially considered some approaches too childish for their students. Conversely, elementary teachers were concerned that some of the techniques were too advanced for their pupils. Both groups were, in most cases, pleasantly surprised by how easily they could adapt approaches for their particular needs.

OVERVIEW

After carefully evaluating the most promising approaches, we wrote this handbook for a broad audience, teachers in any type of classroom where bilingualism plays a role. It contains six chapters.

Chapter 1 outlines current notions of literacy and explains the complexities of bilingualism and the process of literacy development for students who function in more than one language or who are learning a second language. Students vary significantly in the way they become bilingual, how they use their languages, what they need to know to be able to read and write, and how their learning is influenced by social and personal factors. Students, then, differ in how they acquire and develop literacy. In tailoring approaches to meet their students' needs, teachers must have the knowledge of and understand the process involved in learning to read and write in more than one language, and their students' unique developmental characteristics.

Chapters 2, 3, and 4 contain 18 different approaches that were successfully employed in elementary and secondary level classes. For each approach, we state the steps for implementation, provide references for further reading, and conclude with an account of how the approach fared in an actual classroom. Case studies illustrate experiences in mainstream, bilingual, ESL, deaf education, and special education classrooms with students of different ages and linguistic and cultural backgrounds. Chapter 2 includes seven approaches that focus on writing, chapter 3 describes approaches helpful for reading development, and chapter 4 presents approaches that support the development of any or all language skills. A few additional approaches are included in Appendix B.

Chapter 5 highlights the essential elements of instruction for bilingual or second-language learners and demonstrates how these approaches provide opportunities for student assessment.

The concluding chapter explains how teachers can improve their instruction by reflecting on students' performance. Based on action research,[6] this chapter illustrates strategies for collecting data, analysis, and reflection. These tasks are deeply embedded in instruction and assessment, making research a natural outcome of good teaching and assessment.

This handbook provides teachers with valuable tools to increase their understanding of bilingual learners in order to maximize instruction. Straightforward explanations of the procedures, which are further illustrated by case studies, allow teachers to use the content of this handbook on their own or in teacher-led study groups. Because of the variety of approaches, teachers can select what best matches their students' needs and their own teaching style.

USING THIS HANDBOOK

Teachers can use this handbook to expand their understanding of literacy and bilingualism, implement literacy approaches and assess student development, and learn through reflection. To build knowledge about literacy, bilingualism, and the development of literacy, we recommend that teachers, in addition to reading the first chapter, read some of the additional sources cited. Teachers should establish students' needs (see the section on learning about your students in chap. 5), choose one or two approaches according to these needs, do additional readings recommended for each approach, and set goals for literacy development. In planning implementation, teachers should also establish assessment strategies to go along with teaching (see chap. 5).

The classroom is ripe with opportunities to learn about literacy development of bilingual learners. Given the idiosyncratic nature of learners, especially when more than one language and culture are involved, observation of student behavior can provide much needed clues as to how to best teach such students. By implementing recommendations in this book, teachers can investigate how

---

[6]See Donahue, Van Tassell, and Patterson (1996); Freeman (1998); and Myers (1985) for information on teacher research.

bilinguals learn, the effect of instruction on their literacy development, or any more specific concerns that emerge from the daily experience of working with students (see chap. 6). Reflection over time is the best way to assess student development. Thus implementation, assessment, and research are deeply connected. Together they can improve teaching and learning.

Teachers can test additional approaches that develop in the future, using the bilingual–bicultural perspective recommended in this handbook. They should also follow the research steps (see chap. 6) in order to explore the effectiveness of the new approach to teach bilingual learners.

Research is an essential component of teacher preparation. To learn how to work with bilingual learners, preservice and in-service teachers must experiment with and reflect on practices recommended in teacher education courses. Direct connection between course content and implementation of practices in a classroom makes for lasting learning and accurate views of how to teach students who are becoming literate in their first language.

LANGUAGE OF LITERACY INSTRUCTION

Literacy instruction of immigrant and language-minority students is often entangled in political battles of language choice.[7] This book is not about in which language to teach literacy, but about how to teach literacy to bilinguals and second-language learners given the language of instruction, be it English, Spanish, French, Japanese, Vietnamese, or others as native or second languages.

There is no question that in U.S. schools the ability to read in English is fundamental to master content area materials. Although some believe that literacy in English is achieved by teaching it directly in English regardless of literacy skills of students, bilingual education programs promote introduction to literacy in the native language of students. Research on literacy of bilinguals has shown that there is high correlation between native language and second-language literacy ability even with languages of dissimilar writing system. There is higher correlation with reading than with writing.[8]

Choice of language for literacy development is closely related to curricular policies, which go beyond the scope of this book. We believe that there are approaches to instruction and assessment that allow bilingual students to develop literacy in their first or second language or both. The classroom context must value and take advantage of the students' linguistic and cultural knowledge. Students must be encouraged to have a positive attitude toward their bilingualism because they perform better when they consider that their bilingual abili-

---

[7]See Brisk (1998a, chap. 1) for a summary of the debate around language and bilingual education.
[8]See Cummins (1991) for a complete review of the literature.

ties help rather than hinder development of their individual languages.[9] Teachers need to understand the interaction between literacy and bilingualism and apply appropriate instructional and assessment practices to enhance the opportunity for successful outcomes.

ACKNOWLEDGMENTS

We have learned much about the recommendations in this handbook from our own students in both teacher education programs and classrooms. We would like to specially thank those teachers who allowed us to use their classroom research and practice to illustrate the teaching approaches included in this handbook, specifically (listed alphabetically): Carmen Alvarez, Angela Burgos, Judy Casulli, Katherine Darlington, Susan Drake, Alice Kanel, Bryna M. Leeder, Musetta Leung, Antolin Medina, Elizabeth E. Morse, Ivelisse Nelson, Renate Weber Riggs, Charles Skidmore, Mary Eileen Skovholt, Milissa Tilton, Laurie Whitten, and Peggy Yeh.

Our special gratitude to Bill Brisk, María's husband, for his consistent feedback throughout the conception and writing of this project. We are grateful to the reviewers whose comments enhanced the quality of this handbook: David Whitenack, San José State University; Concepción Valadez, University of California at Los Angeles; and James Flood, San Diego State University. Special gratitude goes to Naomi Silverman, our editor, who assisted and facilitated the process with much grace.

---

[9]Hakuta and D'Andrea (1992) and Jimenez, García, and Pearson (1995) observed this phenomenon in their research.

About the Authors

María Estela Brisk is a professor at the Lynch School of Education, Boston College. Her research and teaching interests include bilingual education, bilingual language and literacy acquisition, and literacy methodology. She is the author of the book *Bilingual Education: From Compensatory to Quality Schooling.* For nearly 20 years, she has taught a course entitled Literacy Development for Bilingual Students to advanced undergraduates and graduate students and in-service teachers. Course participants not only employ approaches included in this handbook in the classroom, they also analyze and report the results.

Margaret M. Harrington is an elementary school teacher with 20 years experience working with bilingual students. She has taught students from second through sixth grade in various types of bilingual programs. She is currently teaching in a combined fourth- and fifth-grade transitional bilingual education classroom in Providence, Rhode Island. For 2 years, she worked in Honduras as a teacher trainer for the Peace Corps instructing teachers on ways to integrate environmental education into their curriculum. Presently, she is a doctoral candidate in the Department of Developmental Studies at Boston University. Her interests are language and literacy development of bilinguals.

1

Literacy and Bilingualism

Teaching literacy to bilingual students requires an understanding of such individuals and the many variables that will affect their performance. Bilinguals function with two or more languages and negotiate more than one culture. Regardless of the language they are using at any time and how well they know it, bilinguals are still influenced by the knowledge of other language(s) as well as by their cross-cultural experience. Bilingual students perfectly fluent in English are different from native speakers of English who do not know another language or have not experienced another culture. The additional and different knowledge they bring to schools must be considered in the teachers' perspective of the students, teaching strategies, and curricular considerations.

The circumstances of literacy acquisition for bilingual students are, in many ways, uniquely individual. Some students are already bilingual when they first encounter the written word and others are literate in their mother tongue when they first learn a second language. The age of the onset of literacy may also vary. Some children start at home before attending school, others develop literacy in kindergarten or first grade, yet others may not start literacy until later due to interruptions in their education.

Becoming biliterate involves learning the linguistic and cultural characteristics of literacy in each language and it requires coping with language and cultural differences. Additionally numerous personal, family, and situational factors affect the performance of bilingual learners. Awareness of what students must learn and the factors affecting them assists teachers working with bilinguals regardless of the curricular content and the language of instruction in their particular classroom.

To prepare themselves to work effectively with bilingual learners teachers must understand the following:

- Literacy development.
- Significance of being bilingual, biliterate, and bicultural.

1

- Interaction between languages in a bilingual learner.
- Knowledge needed to read and write.
- Factors affecting literacy development.

LITERACY DEVELOPMENT

Literacy has been defined from different viewpoints, all of which contribute to understanding literacy development among bilinguals. Literacy has been defined in relation to context and process. "Literacy is control of secondary uses of language (i.e., uses of language in secondary discourses)."[1] Primary discourses serve for communication among intimates who share a great deal of knowledge such as family, friends, and neighbors. Secondary discourses are those used in institutions such as schools, stores, workplaces, government offices, churches, and businesses. Literacy's functions differ according to institutional contexts. Schools require academic papers, logical discussion of issues, and comprehension of academic texts of various disciplines. In stores, literacy serves mainly for labeling and pricing. Interpreting memoranda and regulations is required in many government offices.

For some bilingual learners, these two discourses are also distinguished by language. The native language often is used only in primary discourses, and secondary discourses occur mostly in the second language. Consequently, bilingual students may not be exposed to the full range of literacy experiences in either language nor have the benefits of smooth transition from familiar to school literacy given that the discourses as well as the languages may be different.

Literacy is also defined as a psycholinguistic process including letter recognition, encoding, decoding, word recognition, sentence comprehension, and so on. Students developing literacy in two languages can learn the psycholinguistic process through one language, but must learn the specific symbol system, words, grammar, and text structure of each language.

Others believe literacy is a social practice that "assumes participation in a community that uses literacy communicatively."[2] The function of literacy may be culturally defined. Differences in schools' uses of literacy may be disconcerting to students who come from a different country. In many schools in the United States, students are expected to participate in discussions of topics incorporating their own ideas, whereas in many Latin American schools, students are expected to recite what they memorized from texts.

Bilingual learners becoming literate must learn how to use literacy in different contexts and for different purposes and how to encode and decode language. They must master these skills for each language and each cultural context.

---

[1]Gee (1989, p. 23).

[2]August and Hakuta (1997, p. 54.) See also Daiute (1985) and Faltis and Hudelson (1998) for additional definitions of literacy.

Literacy is developmental (i.e., children get better at it with time and experience). The language for secondary discourse may start developing at home through conscious efforts of parents or family members. Literacy development at school is then a continuation and enhancement of efforts started at home. Sometimes parents inculcate their children to literacy practices familiar to them from when they went to school, which may no longer be advocated by the school.[3] Mutual adjustment and understanding between home and school practices greatly enhances and facilitates literacy acquisition.[4]

Learners acquire literacy from exposure to authentic texts in authentic situations. Home and public places contain much written language that becomes familiar to children. However, for some children, words they see in the environment may not be in the language they know and therefore, this written language does not assist in the natural process of literacy acquisition. An English-speaking parent can seize opportunities to teach reading while pouring juice from a bottle with the label *apple juice*, while crossing streets attending to the *walk/don't walk* signs, or while reading with the child the name of the animals listed on the cages at the zoo. Parents who speak other languages usually lack such literacy support for their languages in their natural environment.

Students also acquire literacy through instruction in the specific psycholinguistic subprocesses. To be able to read or write, students must learn and develop automaticity in such skills as letter and word recognition, encoding, and decoding. Bilinguals learn such skills in both languages. Although they may be able to apply the process and strategies learned in one language to their new language, they still need to learn specific characteristics in each language.

BILINGUAL, BILITERATE, BICULTURAL

There are many reasons why students become bilingual. Immigrant children need to learn the new country's language. Deaf children learn English as a second language when they start to read and write. English-speakers learn other languages in school or as sojourners[5] in foreign countries. Some children are raised speaking more than one language. Thus, bilingual students are defined by their experience with more than one language and culture and not by attendance in a bilingual education program.[6]

"Bilinguals know more than one language to different degrees and use these languages for a variety of purposes."[7] They may understand, speak, read, and

---

[3]Goldenberg, Reese, and Gallimore (1992) illustrated how parents focused on teaching children phonics, whereas the school advocated a whole language approach to literacy.

[4]Saravia-Shore and Arvizu (1992) contains many studies illustrating literacy in the home and school.

[5]Sojourners are children of businessmen or professionals who stay temporarily in the country.

[6]For more extensive readings on bilingualism see Grosjean (1982, 1989), Lyon (1996), McLaughlin (1984), and Romaine (1995).

[7]Brisk (1998a, p. xvi).

write their languages very well, or they might be in the process of developing any of the language skills in either of the languages. The use of each language can vary from casual daily conversation to academic uses. Proficiency and use are closely interrelated because proficiency facilitates use and use promotes proficiency. Levels of proficiency and amount of use change for each language throughout the life of a bilingual. Intensive exposure to a second language, as in the case of immigrant children or sojourners, disrupts development of the native language, which may become their weaker language. Some students study this language when they reach high school, regaining fluency.

Biliteracy is "the acquisition and learning of the decoding and encoding of and around print using two linguistic and cultural systems in order to convey messages in a variety of contexts."[8] Bilinguals can have different degrees of biliteracy. When evaluating literacy of bilingual students it is important to distinguish between literacy (i.e., being able to function as a literate person in either language), and specific proficiency to read and write in a particular language. A group of first graders are at grade level in literacy, as well as in proficiency, in both languages if they read at grade level in both languages. On the other hand, if eighth graders read at first-grade level in English, while they can read eighth-grade content-area books in Chinese, they have an eighth-grade level of literacy, but only a first-grade level reading proficiency in English.

Literacy skills are acquired only once through one language and then applied to the new language. Thus, literacy ability in one language supports the acquisition of literacy in another.[9] Learners who recognize the benefits of knowing one language in acquiring literacy skills in the other become more proficient in literacy skills in the second language.[10]

Because languages are not alike, learners need to acquire the idiosyncrasies of the new language. Literate students have the concept of decoding, know that different genres require different text structures, and so on. They do not have to learn everything, just the subtleties that distinguish the languages. Different languages have different rules. Although business letters written in Spanish and in English will have a heading, body, and salutation, the organization of the body greatly differs. A letter written by a Latin American will start with something personal to establish a relationship before going to the business matter. When composing a letter, an American will go straight to the purpose of the letter.

Students acquiring literacy in two languages simultaneously may learn literacy skills through either and then apply them to the opposite language. For example, Arabic students in Israel learning to write in both Arabic and Hebrew learned the process approach to writing in their Hebrew as a second language class and then applied these skills to writing in Arabic.

---

[8]Pérez and Torres-Guzmán (1996, p. 54).

[9]See Cummins (1991) for an extensive review of the literature.

[10]Jimenez, Garcia, and Pearson (1995) illustrated the difference in literacy achievement between a student who believed both her languages helped and one who did not.

Bilinguals' knowledge of the cultures and ability to function in the cultural contexts of these languages vary greatly. Contact with a new culture challenges once firmly held beliefs and behaviors. Some bilinguals flow naturally between the cultures, whereas others may reject one of the cultures.

Culture influences literacy uses and values, prior knowledge, text organization, and connotation of words. Students learn the uses and values of literacy from their experiences in their culture. When confronted with another culture, they need to learn and understand new values and solve possible conflicts.[11] For example, Christina, an English as a Second Language (ESL) teacher, was always amazed at her Vietnamese students' concern for their penmanship. Penmanship is a highly valued component of literacy within the Vietnamese education.

Bilingual students bring to the class all the knowledge acquired through their cultural experiences. These relate both to the parents' ancestral culture and the students' own life experiences. When the content of texts or the topics of writings are familiar and interesting to learners, they are more successful in reading and writing. When students are working in their second language, choosing familiar topics can have a dramatic effect on their performance. For example, a group of sixth-grade immigrant students who had been characterized by their mainstream teacher as timid and with limited English proficiency, surprised their teacher and English-speaking colleagues when they read and discussed the book *Guests* and wrote about their own experiences as immigrants. With experience and increased language knowledge, students can then venture into writing about new and less familiar topics.

Culture dictates the organization of text.[12] When asked to provide a written description of their students, a Mexican teacher wrote an essay containing factual information as well as her feelings toward the children; a Korean teacher provided a succinct, numbered list of characteristics; and an American teacher wrote a factual description. Biliterate writers need to understand the cultural context of their audience to determine the text structure they need to use. Biliterate readers need to understand the cultural context of the writer to set their expectations for text organization.

Word connotations are defined by the cultural context. Students who do not know the culture miss the full meaning of words. When asked to give associations to the word *creature*, a group of Japanese students gave the word *being*. In the reading, the author's intended meaning was of a *monster*. The Japanese students lost the sense of the sentence by not knowing this added meaning often used in the American culture.

Being bilingual, biliterate, and bicultural is a balancing act that needs support from teachers and families. Often students feel that one language is competing with the other rather than assisting it. Obtaining fluency and accuracy in

---

[11]Pérez (1998) illustrated the differences in sociocultural contexts for a variety of cultural groups.
[12]Connor and Kaplan (1987) contains a number of studies on structure of text and cultures.

two languages is hard work, but it can be highly beneficial in a world of increasing multilingual encounters. For students who live a bilingual reality it is best to nurture both languages and cultures.

INTERACTION BETWEEN THE LANGUAGES

Language choice, codeswitching, and the use of both languages when performing literacy activities, regardless of the language of the text, are natural phenomena among bilinguals. The fact that bilinguals use both languages is not evidence of confusion, but just the tapping of their linguistic resources. Bilinguals choose a particular language to speak, read, or write for a variety of reasons: level of proficiency, specific topic, characteristics of their audience, setting, motivation to practice a language, and so on. Diego,[13] a high school student, wrote dialogue journals in his computer class. Because the teacher only spoke English, he would start his journal entries in English, saying as much as he could. Then he would switch to Spanish to expand on the topic and say all those things he could not express as well in English.

Codeswitching is the alternate use of two languages.[14] These switches can occur within the discourse, where the person starts in one language and then switches to the other, between sentences, or even within sentences when only a phrase or word is in the other language. *Language switching,* which is more common in the oral than in the written language, is not random, but rather, governed by functional and grammatical rules. The reasons for this switching are many and well documented. It can simply be that a word comes more readily in one language, a topic is easier to discuss in one language, there is a desire to express an added meaning by changing language, or the student has no equivalent expression in the other language. Eva wrote a paper in Spanish using an occasional word in English: "Algunos viernes tenemos *girl scouse*, música, ciencia … " (Fridays we have Girl Scouts, music, science …). Her experience with Girl Scouts has been only in the United States, so she does not have an equivalent in Spanish.

Formal texts may switch languages to establish the cultural identity of a character. The children's book *Sing, Little Sack* is a story written in English about a Puerto Rican girl. Spanish is used occasionally to highlight the child's culture. For example, the lullaby her mother sang to her as a child, as well as expressions such as *mi niña* (my child) and *mamá* (mother), appear in Spanish.

Literacy ability in a second language flourishes in environments where the use of the native language is supported. Bilingual students can often explain better in their native language the contents of a reading done in their second language. They may also find it helpful to discuss and plan writing in their

---

[13]The names of all students mentioned in this handbook have been changed for confidentiality.
[14]Romaine (1995) explained extensively the phenomenon of codeswitching.

stronger language, although the product is in their second language. When writing in a second language, students may switch to their native language to avoid interrupting the flow of what they want to say for lack of language proficiency. For example, Allison wrote dialogue journals with her high school French teacher. She wrote as much as she could in French, but when missing a word or structure she would switch to English: "*Last night*, nous avons aller a *Spooky World*. Il est tres *scary, and fun*." As students develop their weaker language, they use it more for reading and writing.

Topic, personality, and attitude toward mixing languages dictate whether bilinguals choose to use their native language or not during literacy activities in the second language. A Ukrainian student used Ukrainian to write about his early childhood experiences, but English to write about his school in the United States. Mabel was very timid and insecure about using English unless she was sure it was correct. Her initial writings included a lot of Spanish. Her brother, on the other hand, showed no fear of using English. His writings were all in English peppered with mistakes.

Even when encouraged to use the native language as a resource, students may refuse to do it. Yuki refused the opportunity to write in Japanese when she got stuck in her English writing. Her teacher was literate in both Japanese and English and could have helped her put into English what she wrote in Japanese. But, Yuki believed that using Japanese was not appropriate in an English lesson.

Learning a new language, like all learning, requires accommodation of new structures into existing ones. Thus, bilinguals do not function as two monolinguals shutting off one language while using the other, but as an integrated individual with two active languages affecting each other and serving as efficient resources for communication.

KNOWLEDGE NEEDED TO READ AND WRITE

Bilinguals need three types of knowledge to become literate in a particular language. They need to know the language, especially the written form of the language; they need to know literacy; and they need to have prior knowledge of the topic. They also need to put all of this knowledge together when reading and writing.[15]

Knowing a language means mastering the structure of text given the genre (i.e., letters, stories, essays, etc.); using words and idiomatic expressions to convey the intended meaning or interpreting words correctly; applying the rules of grammar to long text, sentences, and words; and using appropriate sound–letter correspondence and orthography. Learners must be aware that written and oral language differ. Level of formality, distance, and cultural

---

[15]Hulstinjn and Matter (1991) contains a number of articles on the knowledge required to read in a second language; O'Malley and Valdez Pierce (1996) explored further the reading process for bilinguals.

norms define the specific characteristics of the written version of the language. In the case of students who use American Sign Language (ASL), the difference is more pronounced because it involves difference in modality, sign versus script, and language, ASL versus English.

Knowledge of literacy from the point of view of a writer includes determining purpose for writing, identifying an audience, establishing the genre, as well as mastering directionality, formatting, mechanics, and punctuation. A reader must master similar skills, but from the opposite perspective, establishing the purpose and organization of the text, the intention of the writer, and understanding the mechanics to be able to decode the text.

Some aspects of language and literacy knowledge are language-specific, whereas others can be applied to both languages. For example, each language has its own vocabulary. Certain words can be very similar in two languages, allowing a bilingual to understand words in the other language. Speakers of Italian, French, Spanish, and Portuguese would have little trouble understanding the English word *language*. Literate Spanish speakers know punctuation symbols, but they need to learn that the exclamation and question marks are only used at the end of a sentence in English and not at the beginning and end as in Spanish. However, literate Japanese speakers need to learn the whole concept, because punctuation is not a characteristic of Japanese written script.

Prior knowledge refers to the concepts and associations (schema) the readers and writers have. Such knowledge includes what they know in general and what their particular cultural knowledge is on a subject. Students may have general knowledge about herbs, but Mexican students may have greater knowledge of their medicinal power. In their culture, herbs are widely used for healing.

Concepts may overlap in the different languages, may be somewhat similar, or be totally different. When the reader and writer come from different cultures, the interpretation of themes may cause difficulties regardless of language proficiency. A third-grade Chinese student was quite capable of reading and understanding a third-grade level story in English about family members who sat down for a lunch of steamed rice. He was quite confused and unable to read when presented with a first-grade level story about children making *rock* stew. His prior knowledge facilitated the comprehension of the former story and not of the latter, even though the language as such was easier in the rock stew story.

In order to read or write, students must bring together simultaneously their knowledge of language, literacy, and concepts. Difficulties in one aspect may affect the performance in the others. Prior knowledge can affect reading comprehension and the ability to compose, regardless of language proficiency. Vicki's high school advanced ESL class voted to write about superstition. Mae, a Chinese student very familiar with this topic, wrote a very well-organized and complete first draft. The writing was interesting and devoid of many language errors. Gennadi, on the other hand, unable to understand the concept, wrote a few sentences that made little sense. Gennadi's lack of prior knowledge affected his language and literacy performance.

Limited knowledge of language can limit students' writing regardless of depth of prior knowledge. Amal's Arabic students had demonstrated ability to write in English in previous lessons, but had great difficulty writing about Ramadan in English. Although they were familiar with the topic, they were not familiar enough with the English vocabulary related to Ramadan to express their ideas in English. Their lack of language affected their written products.

Limited knowledge of vocabulary and lack of cultural knowledge make the reading of social studies texts difficult for literate bilingual students. It is not uncommon for the authors of such texts to use various words and phrases to mean the same thing. Choua, a sixth-grade Hmong student, was quite confused and exasperated while studying about the American Revolution. She explained to her teacher that she understood that the British were fighting the Colonists, but could not figure out who those "Red Coats" were, and for whom they were fighting. Success in literacy activities not only depends on literacy skills, but also on the development of language as well as cultural knowledge needed to cope with the variety of texts to which students are exposed in schools.

FACTORS AFFECTING LITERACY DEVELOPMENT

Contextual and personal variables affect the process of literacy development and the level of achievement of bilingual students. For this reason, bilingual students develop literacy skills at different rates, including different rates for each language. Therefore, teachers need to know and understand each student individually and be aware of their literacy level in each language.

Contexts of literacy development include factors in the society at large, the school, and the home of the students. Bilinguals may become literate in an environment where they are exposed to two or more languages, or in a monolingual environment where everything is mostly in one language, but through instruction they acquire another language.

Sara, María, and Angélica were exposed to English and Spanish literacy since childhood. Sara is equally proficient in both languages, whereas Angélica's English far surpasses her Spanish. María, although fully proficient in English still makes occasional errors in writing typical of second-language learners. Differences in external factors contributed to their difference in abilities. Sara was raised in Florida and was exposed equally to both languages at and outside school; Angélica grew up in New England where she attended schools where the instruction was only in English. She was exposed to literacy in Spanish at home and during her occasional visits to Latin America. María lived in Latin America until she was an adult, where she studied English from preschool through college.

The amount of environmental literacy in each language both at home and outside the home, as well as the status and economic viability of the languages, support or hinder motivation to learn to read and write in specific languages. The type of writing system, status of the languages, and whether they have been standardized, shape attitudes about difficulty or worth of learning specific languages.[16] Both Sara and María lived in environments where knowledge of both languages was highly desirable for social and economic reasons. Usefulness and status of Spanish in New England is not comparable to English. Angélica's motivation came from within the family, not the society.

Language characteristics influence and restrict educational decisions with respect to developing literacy in home languages. Spanish is an efficient language to teach children to read. With appropriate instruction and materials, students can master reading within the first couple of grades. The writing system is similar enough to English to establish a strong foundation to acquisition of written English. In an educational environment that pressures bilingual programs to transfer students as quickly as possible, Spanish allows programs to have students reading in Spanish before switching completely to English. Other languages present different challenges. For example, Chinese is not only a very different writing system than English, but it takes much longer to learn it. In China, not until sixth-grade do students master enough written Chinese to read a newspaper.[17] Teaching reading to Chinese bilinguals and its implications on bilingual education policies have to be seen in a different light than those for Spanish speakers.

Home literacy habits, attitudes toward literacy and languages, perceptions of the function of literacy, and uses of literacy in specific languages influence the children's attitude, motivation, and proficiency. A survey that Lisa, a mainstream teacher, carried out with the families of her Asian and Spanish-speaking students revealed similarities and differences between ethnic groups as well as between families. Asian children tended to be read to by older siblings, whereas Spanish speakers were read to by their parents. Religious topics were common reading material among Spanish-speakers. Both groups had some families that were more invested than others in their literacy practices at home.

Families' concept of literacy and their practices may be congruent with the school, may be very different from the school's,[18] or may be a combination of beliefs.[19] Level and quality of communication and understanding between home and school influences students' acquisition of literacy.

---

[16]See Brisk (1998a, chap. 2) for a complete account of factors influencing bilingual students.
[17]See Leong (1978) for teaching reading in Chinese.
[18]Heath (1983) described families that carried out literacy practices congruent with the school's and those whose practice greatly differed from those of the school.
[19]Duranti and Ochs (1995) described a bicultural approach to literacy development in the home of Samoan children.

Schools influence students' achievement by the effectiveness of approaches used to teach literacy, teacher expectations, and specific languages promoted.[20] Students will experience more favorable learning conditions in contexts where the languages they are learning are used and the attitudes toward them are positive. Respect for the students' own language, even if it is not used for instruction, favors learning because it reflects respect for the students themselves and their families.

Personal variables include age, when the languages were learned, level of proficiency in the languages, cultural norms for language use, when literacy in each language was introduced, level of literacy ability, educational background, and attitudes toward the languages.[21]

Personal variables affect the individuals directly and interact with the social variables to make the learning conditions more or less favorable for general literacy development and for proficiency in particular languages. Gabriel is a high school student born in the United States of Puerto Rican parents. He can speak Spanish well enough to get along in his community, but is unable to read or write in it and unwilling to learn. He speaks, reads, and writes English fluently, although his academic achievement in school does not reflect superior levels of literacy. Educational background and attitudes shaped Gabriel's Spanish proficiency and unwillingness to improve his Spanish. Lack of formal schooling in Spanish prevented him from learning to read and write in Spanish. Gabriel also has a confused attitude toward Spanish. Although he claims it is useful to be bilingual, he quietly refuses to cooperate in his Spanish-language class. The society at large and school pressure Gabriel to embrace English and not value his Spanish heritage. On the other hand, his family tells him he is Puerto Rican. Thus, the root of Gabriel's inability to decode in Spanish cannot be found in literacy, but in Gabriel's life story.

CONCLUSION

Becoming bilingual, biliterate, and bicultural is desirable for students who have the opportunity or the need to experience more than one language and culture. It is not, however, an easy accomplishment. The students' individual characteristics in interaction with the environment help or hinder the process. Teachers who want their students to succeed in literacy learning must accept the students' bilingualism and understand the complexity of biliteracy. They need to assist these students' literacy development by building literacy, language, cultural knowledge, and a positive attitude toward their bilingualism. The advantages of high levels of bilingualism justify fomenting it in schools. Schools that are not equipped to instruct students in two languages can still encourage students to continue development of their other languages.

---

[20]For full explanation of these variables, see Brisk (1998a) and Mackey (1968).
[21]Brisk (1998a) and Lyon (1996) contain more detailed explanations of these variables.

2

Approaches
With Focus on Writing

The teaching of writing has undergone many changes. Older students and parents may not be familiar with the new approaches that allow experimenting and creativity. Teachers need to help students transition to the new ways of learning to write and be clear to parents about their approach and goals. The approaches included in this section help students develop and practice their writing in meaningful ways. There is much opportunity for oral expression (or singing), and reading, as well. Some writing approaches include the following:

- Mailbox Game
- Drawing as Prewriting
- Dialogue Journal
- Talk–Write
- Process Writing
- Process Writing: Computers
- Show Not Tell

The Mailbox Game and Drawing as Prewriting are particularly useful approaches for beginners to the writing process. Even older students have enjoyed letter writing and drawing as a way to help expression when working in a second language. It took Debbie, a high school foreign language teacher, much effort to convince her students that drawing was not childish, but in the end, Drawing as Prewriting proved very helpful for her beginner students. Several teachers have combined Drawing as Prewriting and Word Cards (see chap. 3) when initiating students to reading and writing.

Dialogue Journals are highly recommended for the first couple of months of the year as a powerful tool to get to know the students and help them lose the fear of writing. Sometimes, students reveal very intimate problems in this written exchange between the teacher and student. Don, an ESL teacher working with Southeast Asian refugees, invited a professional counselor to the class to discuss the traumas that students were noting in their journals.

Dialogue Journals are harder to use when the teacher and student do not share a language. Teachers can be creative in their adaptations. Lori told a recently arrived Vietnamese student to draw instead of write in his journal. In her response she explained in English what she thought the drawing was about, thus giving him vocabulary for the things he wanted to express.

The Talk–Write approach is an excellent way to develop initial drafts and give students practice in being critical and helpful about each other's work. It is a useful approach to implement prior to Process Writing, because it focuses on the development and clarity of topic. It can also be helpful when students have different strengths. A mainstream teacher paired José, a Spanish-speaker fluent in oral but not written English, with a native speaker of English. José acted as the questioner, leaving for the native speaker the role of modeling the oral and written language.

Process Writing is a comprehensive way to develop writing. It is good to use after the other approaches that have eased the students into writing. Process Writing allows for more explicit teaching than Dialogue Journal or Talk–Write. The ability to improve each writing project increases with time. Using the computer allows students to revise more than once without having to rewrite all over again. The Rhetorical Approach (see Appendix B) breaks the planning stage of process writing into very clear steps. It can be very helpful for more advanced writers. Show Not Tell is a very specific strategy to improve something the students have already written. It helps students develop rich expression and should be coordinated with Process Writing.

MAILBOX GAME

Purpose

The Mailbox Game gives a real-life context for the children's natural desire to write each other notes in class. Letter writing provides an opportunity for the students to write for a genuine purpose to a specific audience. In a bilingual classroom, students are given the freedom of language choice. When used in a second-language context, students are able to work at their individual levels of proficiency. It allows all students to communicate with each other and get to know each other, helping in the formation of a classroom community.[1]

---

[1]See Peregoy and Boyle (1996) for further information on this approach.

Materials

Materials for the Mailbox Game include the following:

1. One large cardboard box made into a mailbox. You can cover it with blue construction paper and put U.S. Mail in red letters. (This step can be skipped with secondary students.)
2. Individual mailboxes for students and teacher (including teacher assistant, student teachers, etc.) with each person's name written on it. This can be done with liquor cartons containing dividers.
3. Note paper, pencils or pens, and some kind of sealer (stapler, gummed stickers, Scotch tape).

Procedure

Procedures for the Mailbox Game include the following:

1. Introduce students to the concept and format of letters. Explain the different options for the salutation and closing of letters.
2. Read books with letter-writing related themes, such as: *The Jolly Postman, Querido Pedrín, Frog and Toad Are Friends, Griffen & Sabine: An Extraordinary Correspondence,* and *Dear Dragon.*
3. Explain to the students that they can write each other letters or notes when they have some free time. They should "mail" them in the large mailbox. You should also write notes or letters, especially if you want to communicate something to the student, such as: "I was sorry to hear that your mother was sick today ... " or "I saw you reading 'x' book, did you like it? ... " Initially, it might be prudent to establish a rule that a student must respond to all letters received to insure that students who write letters in turn receive letters.
4. One student is nominated the mail carrier (for the day or the whole week). At a set time, the "mail carrier" delivers the letters to the boxes with the appropriate name. This should be done while the other students are busy working on something else.
5. Allow students to pick up their mail without disrupting other activities, for instance, after lunch, or snack (just as people do when working in an office, and so forth).

If students have trouble reading because they are beginners, they can ask the author for clarification. You should not correct spelling or anything else in these letters. If students want to ask how to write something, you can help or teach them how to use the dictionary.

The Approach in Practice: You've Got Mail![2]

Milissa implemented the Mailbox Game with a fourth-grade two-way Spanish–English bilingual classroom. The students were a mixture of native English-speakers and native Spanish-speakers who had been together in the two-way bilingual program since kindergarten. She felt that this form of writing would allow the students the opportunity to write for a real purpose on topics that they had chosen to an audience that they had selected. She also believed that it would satisfy their natural desire to communicate with each other and provide an opportunity for building and fostering relationships within the classroom. The educational goals for the project included encouraging better friendships and relationships among classmates, helping students express themselves through writing; improving writing skills, and encouraging students to take more risks in writing creatively and with more details.

Milissa introduced the idea of the Mailbox game to the students. She explained that by writing letters they might get to know their classmates better, and learn the process of letter writing in a purposeful and fun way. The elements of letter writing (date, salutation, body, closing, etc.) were explained to the students. Appropriate and inappropriate topics were also discussed. Students were encouraged to write in both English and Spanish. Samples of letters were written in both languages and displayed on a bulletin board. The single rule established in the program was that if a person received a letter from someone, he or she was obligated to return a letter to that person.

A different person was chosen each week to be the mail deliverer, another to stamp the letters. Class meetings were held weekly so that the students could ask questions about or voice opinions of the Mailbox Game. One student immediately expressed his unwillingness to participate in the project. Milissa encouraged him to try, but did not pressure him into joining the activity.

For a majority of the day, except for lunch, recess, and a 20-minute journal writing period first thing in the morning, the 37 students were divided into two groups (Latitude and Longitude), each working with a teacher. While one group was being instructed in Spanish, the other was working in English, then they alternated. Students did a lot of collaborative group work. For the Mailbox Game, the students were encouraged to write to someone in the group to which they did not belong (i.e., someone from Latitude would write to someone from Longitude).

Letter writing was scheduled as a homework project. However, very quickly it became apparent that some time was needed during the school day for students to write the letters. Students complained that they did not have time after school to write letters because they were busy with homework and other activities. The students were then allowed to work on their letters during the

---

[2]This project was carried out by Milissa Tilton.

20-minute journal writing period. Later, when students became enthusiastic about the project, they wrote letters both during and after school.

The students were given a week to write the letters. Forty-three letters were written during the first week. The teachers made sure that everyone had received at least one letter. If a student did not have a letter, a teacher wrote to the student. Later on, when the mail carriers noticed that some students had not received a letter, they wrote one to them, so their feelings were not hurt.

The students wrote about many topics: friendship, qualities that made the person a good friend, memories of time shared together, music, TV shows, and sports. Elizabeth wrote a letter to Vilmaris about activities that were happening in the class. She was very excited about the duck eggs that were going to hatch. She also wrote about a contest the class was having on naming the capitals of the states, and explained how she was going to try to learn all the capitals.

Most of the letters written that week were in English, however, four were written in Spanish by native Spanish-speakers, and two were written in Spanish by native English-speakers. The letters written by the native English-speakers were addressed to native speakers of Spanish. These students were aware of their audience and had decided to write in that person's first language.

Although errors in the letters were not corrected, Milissa did comment to the class as a whole on the content of the letters, appropriate styles, complete addresses, dates, and salutations. She encouraged the students to refer to the bulletin board display that showed samples of letters and addresses in both languages.

As the weeks progressed, the number of letters sent and received increased. In the eighth week of the project, 132 letters had been written. The students showed progress in selecting topics, increasing creativity, and in the general length of their letters. Some students included poems in their letters, or verses from favorite songs, and another student reflected on the math lesson of the day and included examples of what he had learned. Students wrote to each other about science projects they were doing, and discussed a book that the class had just finished reading. Some students began to personalize their stationery with stickers, stamps, and colorful decorations. Other students wrote letters on their computers at home. Enthusiasm for writing the letters was high. Some students came to school without their homework, but had written a letter! The student who had initially refused to write letters, finally in the seventh week, after having received a letter from a teacher, wrote back to the teacher, and then to eight other students. Apparently, the enthusiasm of the other students receiving letters had shown him that the only way to get letters was to write them.

The students improved in both their technical aspects of letter writing as well as writing in general. Milissa set the expectation of high standards by reminding students of proper letter-writing techniques during the project. Some of the students also helped each other by writing about grammar mistakes found in letters. Ed, in particular, showed a marked improvement in his format.

When first writing his letters, he did not use a salutation, closing, or date. After a few lessons on letter-writing formats, Ed began to include the opening and closing sections to his letters. By the end of the 8-week project, most of the letters sent by the students had the date and a proper salutation and closing.

The Mailbox Game was a wonderful opportunity for the students to improve friendships, establish new ones, and increase sensitivity to others. A new friendship was formed between a native Spanish-speaking boy and a native English-speaking boy who had not socialized with each other previously. They wrote faithfully to each other in 7 of the 8 weeks, sharing information about each other and their families. Two girls, one native Spanish-speaker and the other a native English-speaker also corresponded, writing half their letter in English and the other half in Spanish. They praised each other for the progress each was making in her second language. Later in the school year, a new student entered the class. She received eight letters from students during her first week telling her how happy they were that she was in their class, inviting her to eat lunch with them and play with them during recess. One girl, who seemed to have difficulty relating socially to the other children in class, was encouraged by letters from the teachers to write to some of the girls in class. She did write to three girls, and then continuously corresponded with them.

Students were able to share joys, problems, and frustrations with each other. At the beginning of the project, one student was writing about her favorite food. By the end, she was writing about moving to a new neighborhood and how the change had affected her. The letter writing also had an influence in some of the students' homes. One mother encouraged her son to begin writing letters to some of his relatives.

The experience was also incorporated into the standard curriculum. Students wrote a business letter to tourist bureaus in different states requesting information on their state. Another letter was sent to museum tour guides thanking them for their assistance on a recent field trip. Some wrote letters while portraying a character from a book they were reading. From the experiences the children had in the Mailbox Game, these "authentic" letters were well written because the students understood to whom they were writing and the purpose of the letter.

At the end of the project, students were asked to reflect on their experiences. Students related that they enjoyed the letter writing because it gave them the opportunity to get to know their friends better. They complained about receiving letters that were messy or not long enough. Some students expressed a feeling of being overwhelmed at times at the number of letters to which they needed to respond. One student suggested that a limit be set for the number of letters sent. Others suggested that each student should write at least once to everyone in the class. Yet others proposed having one partner with whom to write back and forth for a scheduled period of time, and then changing to another person.

The Mailbox Game can be contagious. One student said that she was going to be a teacher when she grew up, and that she would like to "steal" the idea of the Mailbox Game. Another student wrote:

> I really like writing letters. I like to write letters, but I like to get them even more. There isn't anything about writing letters that I don't like. Sometimes I do not have enough time to write, but I try. I start the letter at home and then I finish it either at home or at school. I think letter writing is a great idea because you get to talk to many different people in the class. Even my mom thinks it's a great idea. She thinks she will do it with her class if that is alright with you.

DRAWING AS PREWRITING

Purpose

Drawing pictures before writing allows the students to get ideas down on paper quickly before they struggle with translating their ideas into written language. Emergent bilingual writers and beginning second-language learners are able to create a story in picture form before committing words to paper and searching for vocabulary that is often unfamiliar to them. As students develop their writing, they naturally skip drawing and write directly. Later, they may add illustrations to their papers.[3]

Procedure

1. Select a general theme. This is best done on what is known about the students and their interests, or related to a field trip, or something that happened that day, or a topic that the class has been discussing. At the early stages, very personal things that are close to the students are best, such as "Me" or "Someone Special." Students can also choose their own themes and work individually or in groups.
2. Prepare a book with blank pages and a cover that suggests the topic. For example, have students draw pictures of themselves, or take a Polaroid picture, and paste it on the cover of the "Me Book." If students are older, they can put the book together after drawing and writing.
3. Brainstorm to decide what will go into the book (can use who, what, when, where, and why questions as a guide). The important aspect of this step is to get the students excited about wanting to draw and write about the topic. They also need to plan to keep the thread of the story.
4. Let students draw their stories on each page. If students have access to graphic software, they can use it for this approach.

---

[3]See Gillespie (1990) and Myers (1983) for further information on this approach.

5. Write captions on each page as the students tell what happened or let them write themselves.
6. Read one or more of the stories to the whole class. Let the students read to each other if they want to do so.

The Approach in Practice: Writing Through Pictures [4]

Susan implemented the Drawing as Prewriting approach with second-grade bilingual students. Of her five students, four were native Spanish-speakers and one spoke Khmer. They were all attending English-only mainstream classrooms, and had been recommended to work with Susan by their classroom teacher. Susan stated that three of the students had been recommended because they were considered bright and deserving of "extra attention." The other two students were sent to Susan because of low academic performance, especially in reading and writing. She felt that the Drawing as Prewriting approach would help these ESL learners, because they would be able to create a story in pictures first that would alleviate problems with immediately thinking about word structure and vocabulary. By drawing pictures first, the students would be able use them as a guide for writing exactly what they wanted to express.

Susan began using the approach by reading to the students a book she had written about herself. They discussed the book and the students then proceeded to fold a paper into a book shape and drew pictures about themselves and their families. Susan purposely did not explain the approach to the students, because she wanted to see what they produced on their own with no pre-stated purpose or introduction. The students were able to write information about themselves modeling some of their ideas after Susan's book, but also including some other personal information about their own families. By having the students write a book about themselves in the first session, Susan was able to learn a bit about each student and the students' backgrounds.

Susan began the second class by reading a passage from *When I was Young in the Mountains* by Cynthia Rylant. She discussed the meaning of memory with the children, and then had them think about their own memories and wrote the students' comments on the board. At first, none of the students could remember anything about their past, until Jonathan remembered his family's Easter celebration. This prompted the other students to remember past family celebrations. This discussion led the students to think about other events with their families. Seroeut remembered a time when he went to the beach and his brother pretended to drown him. Then, Jonathan spoke about a mountain climbing trip he took during winter vacation.

With some assistance from Susan for ideas, each student began to draw a picture of something that had happened to him or her in the past and then wrote

---

[4]This project was carried out by Susan M. Drake.

something to go with the drawing. It was still difficult for two of the students, Nestor and Elvin, who did not seem to grasp the idea of drawing about an actual event. Elvin had drawn a helicopter, but when Susan asked if he had ever been in one, he responded that he had not. After a discussion with Susan about his vacation, he began drawing a picture of a baseball game he played with his cousin.

When she first started using the approach, the students orally told elaborate stories to go with their drawings, but only wrote one or two simple sentences that often did not seem to match their drawings. This discrepancy seemed to dissipate over time as the students gradually were able to use their drawings to help write their stories. Alex, for example, had very limited verbal skills in English. However, when he was able to draw a picture first, then describe what was happening in it, he was able to develop more complex sentences and coherent stories. He needed the drawing to help him develop his written ideas.

During the sessions, the students were allowed and often encouraged to share and discuss their ideas and stories with each other. When they first began the project, they were reluctant to talk or work together. They did not seem to understand the value of sharing ideas. They often covered their papers and would not let anyone, except Susan, see what they had drawn or written. Two students, Alex and Nestor, especially had difficulty working together. They were both brainstorming ideas about animals, but did not want to help each other with those ideas. Gradually, both boys began to see the positive aspects of working out ideas together. Several weeks into the project, the students were doing so well coming up with their own topics and ideas, that they sometimes rejected those suggested by Susan.

The students also had difficulty listening to the texts written by their classmates and contributing helpful comments about the work. Elvin was the first student to read his story. Susan modeled a response to Elvin's story, commenting on what she had liked about it, hoping that another student would want to add something. This, however, did not happen, and Susan had to ask the other students for their opinions. Sarouet offered a suggestion, but the other students had nothing to say. They seemed more concerned with working on their own stories and did not welcome comments or suggestions from the others.

Susan found that the process of sharing ideas and offering helpful comments grew as the students became more confident in their abilities to create their own topics and stories. In one such instance, Elvin did not seem to understand what he had to do. Sarouet showed Elvin his own list of ideas, and then made several suggestions to Elvin, including topics that Sarouet knew would interest his friend, such as Ninja Turtles. Elvin happily began writing his list, and even contributed ideas to other students.

Eventually, the students were able to offer constructive comments to each other, and the writers listened. After one person finished reading his or her story, each of the other students commented on something they liked about it, and offered a suggestion for a change or addition. The author then decided which, if any, of the suggestions would be used to improve the story.

Susan observed a natural shift from drawing as the precursor to writing, to drawing done second to writing. She noted that when she first began working with the students, all five started their stories by drawing first. Gradually, three of the five students wrote their stories first and then illustrated them. The written word replaced drawing as the initial symbol of ideas. For Alex, however, drawing was still needed to help him create ideas, although he was better able to elaborate in his writing. Susan also noticed an increase in sentences and more complex sentence structure in the stories of all the children as the sessions continued.

The growth in the ability to read and decode words was also developed during the drawing as prewriting sessions. Because Alex was unable to write the words for his stories, he dictated them to Susan. He was not able to read the words back to her, even though they were written exactly as he had dictated them and he did know the sounds for many of the letters. Susan decided to use the Word Card approach (see chap. 3) with Alex and another boy, Nestor, to see if that might help improve their sound–symbol reading ability. Alex did improve his reading ability as time went on. During one of the last sessions, he was able to read his story aloud. He even commanded two of the other students to sit down and listen to him. When he encountered problems in reading some words, the other children crowded around him to help.

This approach proved helpful to all the students in different ways. Some of the students were able to further develop their abilities to select topics and elaborate on their ideas. For others, like Alex, drawing as prewriting provided a means to help develop ideas first in a nonverbal way, so that writing down the ideas later became easier.

DIALOGUE JOURNALS

Purpose

The Dialogue Journal acts as a bridge between oral interaction and the development of composing by providing the student the opportunity of a written conversation with a teacher. The journal provides a natural, purposeful means of writing for the student. There are no requirements regarding topic and the student's writing is not corrected or evaluated. The normal unequal status of teacher and student is minimized, because both parties are equally engaged in the interaction, introducing and elaborating on topics, and so forth. One person does not dominate or control the interaction with directives and questions. The teacher is involved in the content of the interaction, as is the student.

This approach is particularly helpful for bilingual learners when they enter a new class because it enhances their relationship with their teacher, and it provides an individual forum for their needs, such as advice on how to deal with the new culture, problems they are having in classes, specific language concerns, and other helpful hints. In a situation in which they have to express themselves in the second language, students are given time to think about appropriate expression. Oral interaction is often too pressured and spontaneous. The flexibility of language use, especially when the teacher is bilingual, and the focus on meaning provides a less stressful communication context.[5]

Materials

Materials needed are a notebook in which students will write, or a disk if using the computer.

Procedure

1. Tell students that:
    a. their Dialogue Journal is a place where they and you will talk about anything they want to talk about;
    b. the journals will not be evaluated or graded in any way;
    c. the journals are private and no one else will read them.
2. Provide each student with a notebook or disk that should be kept in the classroom.
3. A brief handout may be given to older students to clarify concepts and any other requirements. For example, you might want to explain that journal writing will help them write better and will not be used for grading purposes; that it is a confidential correspondence between the two writers. You can also include some basic instructions such as including the date on all entries or writing on only one side of the paper. Some teachers require a minimum number of lines be written.

    If teaching an elementary self-contained class, have students read their journals (your responses to their previous entries) first, then give them time to write their responses. Allow them to return to the journal during the day if they have more to say to you. For high school students, journal writing can be done in class or for homework.
4. Encourage students to write to you about real issues that are important to them, seeking or giving genuine information, solving problems, and so forth. Participants are free to choose topics as they become important, without fear of censure. You should never predetermine the topics.
5. Communicate frequently and continuously, at least once a week for at least a couple of months. Although, every day for the whole academic year is optimal, it should be done only as frequently as it is possible to respond to students. Don't overdo it.

---

[5]See Freeman and Freeman (1989), D'Angelo Bromley (1989), Kreeft Peyton (1990), Reyes (1991), and Stanton (1988) for further information about this approach.

6. Keep the communication private. This will help students feel free to express themselves and not fear correction or exposure. Journals become confidence builders and emotional outlets for students experiencing difficulties.
7. Your responses should show interest in what the students have to say. Focus on meaning, not form. Do not correct when responding. It is better to write short responses with few questions. Seek only to clarify meaning. You should ask questions when meaning is unclear. You may model in your responses the correct form of mistakes that appeared in students' entries.

The Approach in Practice—Getting to Know You: Dialogue Journals in Middle School Classroom[6]

Dialogue Journal writing was done by Katherine's seventh- and eighth-grade Transitional Bilingual Education (TBE) class. The students, who were all native Spanish-speakers, were at various levels of English proficiency. Katherine felt that Dialogue Journals would help her students write for purposeful reasons. Additionally, because her students were at many different levels of English proficiency, Katherine believed that dialogue journals would allow her to individualize the English learning needs of each student.

Katherine introduced Dialogue Journals to her students and explained that they would be writing in the journals twice a week. They were told that they could write about anything, and could write as much as they wanted as long as they had written at least five lines. The students were free to write in either English or Spanish. She responded to the journal entry in the same language. Initially, Katherine scheduled 10 minutes for the journal writing, but soon discovered that some students needed more time to write, so she created a more flexible schedule, allowing students to write for a longer period of time. Those students who finished early worked on an assignment quietly so that the journal writers could continue uninterrupted. Katherine found that the best time for her students to write in their journals was early morning because they were more enthusiastic and there were fewer interruptions. This also allowed her time during the day to respond to the journal entries.

Most of the students were interested in writing in the journals, some even expressing dismay at not being able to finish them in the allotted time. It was for this reason that Katherine allowed students who wanted to continue to do so while other students worked silently for a time on other assignments. Students were also able to write, if they so desired, at other times during the day.

Katherine enthusiastically read all the journal entries that first night. She reported that the next day several students greeted her and stopped to talk before

---

[6]This project was carried out by Katherine Darlington.

school. She felt as if the students were more trusting of her because she now knew something secret about them, and yet she was still there smiling at them, accepting them for who they were.

The students' development during journal writing varied. Some students seemed to enjoy the process and their entries became longer and more focused, whereas others were still hesitant to share more personally even after several weeks. Katherine did observe that, through her responses to the journal entries, some students were able to write in a more personal, meaningful way. For example, one of the students had only written, "Sorry, have nothing to write." Katherine responded:

> Do you know I was really surprised to hear you reading in Science today.
>
> Your English is improving very quickly.
>
> How do you like your new seating assignment?

The student's next journal entry was as follows:

> I like it, thank you for changing because I was angry with Sharon. and I was going to get in trouble, if I stay near her.

Some students changed from always complaining about something to asking personal, thoughtful questions of Katherine. One student wrote:

> What will you say if your sun [son] was in this shichashon [situation] you wont tell him the same thing yes or no—why.

Another student was able to talk about problems she was experiencing since her mother had left home. This student had never spoken to Katherine on such a personal level.

Katherine did an analysis of the topics covered by the students in their journals. The journals were used to question, inform, request, apologize, thank, and report. Results showed that students wrote most about peer and family relationships and self-reflection. Family situations were the most prevalent, followed by conflicts or misunderstandings among friends. They also addressed school subjects, highlights of their school day, and other topics related to their own lives.

The students were asked to complete an evaluation of the Dialogue Journal approach. The evaluation was divided into three parts: self-evaluation, assessment of method, and assessment of teacher's responses. Students indicated that they had learned something from the Dialogue Journals. Many expressed the positive experiences of journal writing such as:

- "getting my feelings out"
- " ... you gave me insights"
- " ... I could tell the thing that happen to me to a person I trust"

- " ... I finally find someone to tell about me and want happen around me"

For the assessment of teacher, Katherine asked the students to evaluate her responses to their entries. Eight students responded that the correspondence was "just about right." Two students felt that Katherine's responses were too short.

In evaluating the success of the method, Katherine felt that the Dialogue Journal approach increased the personal interactions and built a higher level of trust between teacher and student. Because the students were allowed to use either Spanish or English, they were better able to communicate effectively. She also felt that she learned a lot about her students through the journals. Katherine also saw attitudinal changes in the students regarding school and peers. For Katherine, the Dialogue Journal approach was an excellent medium of meaningful, functional communication.

TALK–WRITE APPROACH

Purpose

This approach gives students the opportunity to talk to someone about what they are writing before committing it to paper. It gives them a real sense of audience. Listeners, by asking questions and offering suggestions, help the writers focus on what they intend to write before actually writing out a story. It is helpful for bilingual and second-language learners because they are able to practice orally what they will later write. By talking to someone before writing, bilingual and second-language learners are able to "work out" vocabulary and linguistic structures that might impede their writing. It also provides a partner in the revision process.[7]

Procedure

1. Pair or let students pair themselves: one will be the talk–writer, the other the questioner.
2. Give them felt pens and large sheets of paper, or have them use a computer.
3. Suggest a topic to write about, have students choose their own, or suggest a broad topic and have pairs choose subtopics.
4. Start the process of talking, writing and reading:
   a. The writers first talk about what they want to write, the questioners encourage, ask questions, seek clarification, and so forth.
   b. Once they feel they have discussed enough, the writers start writing. The questioners help the writers include all information and or-

---

[7]See Zoellner (1983) and Wixon and Wixon (1983) for further information about this approach.

ganize thoughts and compose the sentences, being careful not to dominate the procedure.

c. When completed, the questioners read the entire piece.

5. Circulate through the groups making suggestions when necessary or providing positive encouragement.

6. When all groups have finished, have students tape products on the wall, point out a few examples that demonstrate positive features of writing, or that may focus on a specific skill that is being taught.

Talk–Write assignments should be short, considered first draft, and not be graded.

The Approach in Practice—That's Right!: Talk–Write Approach for Bilingual ASL Students

For Paul's[8] students, the Talk–Write approach proved to be a helpful tool for improving the depth and clarity of their oral and written summaries and reports. Paul, a bilingual English–ASL teacher, adapted the Talk–Write approach for four students (ranging in age from 16 to 18 years old) in his "substantially separate" English class in a public high school. The students are with Paul for 45 minutes each day. During other periods, the students are in mainstreamed classes with 25 to 30 hearing students, a content-area teacher, and a sign language interpreter. Two of the students, Debbie and Lakeysha, are profoundly deaf. They are both bilingual in ASL and English, although Paul stated that they are not completely fluent in ASL, and use a type of sign language called Pidgin Signed English (PSE) when they speak to each other in his English class. Both Debbie and Lakeysha are reading below grade level (fourth-grade reading level on standardized testing) and have trouble with vocabulary and grammatical elements in writing.

Another student, Briana, has a mild hearing loss. Her reading comprehension is good, and she has good control of English grammar and syntax. Her main area of difficulty in writing is developing and organizing her thoughts. The fourth student, Robert, is hearing, but has a history of severe language delays. Because of the language problems, Robert attended a school for deaf students and learned sign language. Robert also demonstrates difficulty in organizing his thoughts when writing.

Paul hoped that by using the Talk–Write approach, the students would see the importance of planning and thinking out what they intended to write before committing to paper. He felt that the approach would help the students to better clarify, redefine, extrapolate, infer, draw conclusions, defend, and debate in

---

[8]Not the real name because we were unable to communicate with the teacher who implemented this approach to obtain permission to use his name.

their writing. He also wanted to change the teacher-directed, teacher-centered writing classes in which these students were used to working.

Paul first tried to incorporate the students' reading lessons into the approach. He had planned to assign readings to the four students and then have them work in pairs, and by using the Talk–Write approach, write summaries of the stories read. Briana and Robert were assigned a chapter from *The Outsiders* to read. They were excited because both had seen the movie version of the book. Debbie and Lakeysha were given a chapter from a book whose main character is deaf. When they met again, Paul found that Briana had not read the chapter that was assigned and was therefore not able to contribute to any discussion or summary of the chapter. She was, however, able to help Robert with his summary by asking questions that helped him expand his ideas and elaborate on the summary.

Similar problems were encountered with Lakeysha and Debbie, who complained that they did not really understand the story they were reading. This experience made Paul realize that the students were probably intimidated by the length and complexity of the stories, and also that they should have been able to choose what they read and wrote about. He then allowed the students to decide on their own writing topics. Both Debbie and Lakeysha expressed interest in reading biographies of deaf people, Briana chose to read about musicians from the *Rolling Stone* magazine, and Robert expressed an interest in writing about "heavy metal" bands. Paul noted that the students were then more willing to work on summarizing the articles they had read. Once the students had read their articles and stories, they worked with each other on the summaries, adapting the Talk–Write approach.

While working with Robert, who had read an article about a musical band, Briana was having difficulty in getting him to express more than the basic factual information obtained from the article. She was finally able to encourage him to reread the article and explain why the band about which he was writing was so famous. Robert was able to write a more comprehensive summary with Briana's assistance. Briana also seemed to have gained something from her experience, because she wanted to take Robert's article home to read!

Debbie and Lakeysha had more difficulty critiquing and offering suggestions to each other's signed summaries. Lakeysha, especially, was not comfortable questioning any of Debbie's remarks. Debbie seemed to have a better idea of what the focus of a biographical summary should be. Lakeysha, on the other hand, was not able to focus on the main point of the biography she read. However, after both Debbie and Lakeysha had reread Lakeysha's article, Debbie was able to help Lakeysha improve her signed summary. Neither of the girls, however, felt comfortable correcting or critiquing each other's written summary. They expected Paul to intervene and correct their writing for them.

Debbie had attended a lecture given by Reginald Redding in which he talked about his experiences of being deaf and African American. For another writing assignment, Debbie chose to write a letter to Reginald Redding. In keeping with the Talk–Write approach, Briana worked with Debbie and helped her organize her thoughts before writing. Debbie told Briana in ASL that she wanted to focus on Mr. Redding's experiences as the only African-American deaf student at a school in New Jersey. Because Briana, acting as the questioner, had not attended the lecture, the questions Briana asked Debbie were authentic. She was seeking information from Debbie that would help her understand the main points of Redding's lecture. Briana asked about Mr. Redding's feelings on being the one African-American deaf student in a school that traditionally educated only White deaf students. She stated that Mr. Redding told them that he had to work very hard. Although Debbie did not seem to want to express her own feelings about the issue when talking to Briana, she did mention them in her letter to Redding.

Debbie wanted to begin her letter by introducing herself; Briana suggested that she include information about the topic of the letter and where Debbie had heard Mr. Redding's talk. Debbie accepted Briana's suggestion and included that information in the first paragraph. In his lecture, Mr. Redding had also spoken about his experiences with racism. Debbie alluded to that in her letter, and was able to relate his experiences to her own as an African-American deaf person. Paul felt that Briana's collaboration with Debbie, through her asking questions and offering suggestions, helped Debbie write the following more comprehensive and meaningful letter:

Dear Reggie Reddish

Hello, my name is Debbie _____, and I went to your lecture about Black History month in Public Boxton liabiry at Copley place. We had been ejoy you in there about black history month. I understand your own past because I almost same experience yours owns about other people rasim to yo also I got too from white people. I am sore tht we had same feel about rasim. now there are change law because of Martin Luther King. Jr. for right now I feel like I am share in world with any people. I only depend on other people is there are good people so I can beam friend with each other thank lord that i am still friend with any peole in the United State.

I am 16 yers old, I am deaf black girl because when I am twenty-two months old, I got high fever i call spinal menigtis. I went though all hearing mate in school only not middle school only deaf and for right now I am in West Roxbury High School it is for hearing mate classroom. also I want to go college and my goal to become a lawyer or psychrlogist or eye doctor. I am not sure because I am in 10th grade now I will be two year later to gradute from high school.

We go visit to Gallaudet college on April 13th and 14th. We want be our guide of M.S.S.D if that okay? Okay thank you for your pleasure to listen us and I hope you will have nice day.

Sincerely

Debbie _____

Lakeysha, who had also attended the lecture, decided to write a summary of Mr. Redding's talk. Unlike Debbie, Lakeysha was not able to incorporate the suggestions of her classmates into her writing. She preferred to sign her ideas to either Debbie or Briana who then wrote them on paper. Once Lakeysha looked over her written ideas, she elaborated and expanded on them using sign language. She still was not comfortable with the writing stage of the Talk–Write approach.

Although each of the four students progressed differently through this Talk–Write approach, Paul believes it helped them all become better writers. He felt that the approach especially helped Lakeysha and Debbie, the two profoundly deaf students, who demonstrated better writing skills when first given the opportunity to express their ideas to others in sign language. This approach also helped students remain on task. When one felt like chatting, the other would remind him or her of the task at hand and the work proceeded in earnest.

PROCESS WRITING

Purpose

The idea behind Process Writing is to get students to write stories, essays, letters, and other types of writing in the way real writers do (i.e., as a process of development from ideas to perfect copy over time and shared with others). For bilingual learners, it allows for flexibility of language use. The students are able to plan using their first language, even if the final product is in the second language. For second-language learners, this approach provides opportunities to develop vocabulary and improve grammar.[9]

Materials

Materials can include plain paper, pencils, typewriters, or computers. Each student and the teacher should have one file folder with his or her name on it. They should be stored together in a place accessible to the students. (If the computer is used, each student should have one diskette with his or her name on it.)

Procedure

Following is the description of the different stages a piece can go through. It is best not to take every piece through all stages. Rather, let students collect drafts and as they get better; they can advance in the stages until they get a few selected pieces written well enough for publishing. Flexibility is necessary because individuals have their own idiosyncratic ways of going about composing.

---

[9]See Boone (1991), Edelsky (1989), Graves (1983), and Lehr (1995) for further information on this approach.

It is better if the teacher also writes to serve as a model for the students. The steps described in the following list help develop good writing habits:

I. Language Choice and Use

Allow students who are beginning to develop writing to choose the language in which they want to write. When students have to write in a particular language, allow them to use either language during planning and drafting to facilitate the flow of ideas. This is especially true when working in a weaker language. For example, when they can't remember a word in one language, they can write it in the other and later look for the equivalent. If they don't know how to start a paper in the second language, let them write it quickly in their native language and then they can try it in their second language. (More proficient speakers usually prefer to do everything in one language.)

II. Genre and Topic Choice

1. Encourage students to write a variety of genres, such as narratives, expository pieces, poems, jokes, letters, songs, plays, and so on.
2. Allow the students to choose their own topics. Alternatively, pairs, groups, or the whole class can write about the same topic.
3. Topics for writing can emerge in a number of ways, such as:
   a. Brainstorm with the class suggestions for topics, write them on the board, overhead, or directly on the computer using a word processing program. You can use the whole list or have the class choose 10 topics about which they think they would like to write. Make a list and paste one copy on the left hand page of each file folder. (If using the computer, copy the file with the list of topics onto each diskette.)
   b. If using Process Writing in connection with content area, choose general topics that must be covered in the content area curriculum, and the students individually, in pairs, or groups, can research and write on one topic. For example, if the general topic is insects, each student researches and writes about one particular insect.
   c. As a follow-up to reading, ask students to write something comparable (e.g., after reading a fable, have students write a story in which one character outsmarts the other).
   d. Ask students to write about the topic that was discussed in a sharing time or discussion session, or related to a field trip.
   e. If your students keep a journal, have them circle topics of interest in their journal and have them write about one.

Any activity that stimulates ideas can then be followed up by writing about it. The less advanced your students are, the less restrictive the topic selection should be. It is easier to write about something the students know and want to express, than about a topic chosen by somebody else that may be unfamiliar or uninteresting to the writer.

III. *Planning for Writing*

Several approaches are good to prepare your students to write a particular piece. This is a time to let the learners speak up about the topic. Ideas should be clarified, vocabulary provided, and further reading may be appropriate. Semantic Mapping, Drawing As Prewriting, reading, researching in the library or through the Internet, interviewing, generating questions, finding answers, sharing time and discussion can all help stimulate ideas, and begin to organize them for the writing. Also, just writing down everything the learner knows about the topic can be an alternative. This step can be done individually, in small groups, or with the whole class. If students have writer's block, talk to them about things you know interest them, have them read something, or listen to other students' pieces.

Help students define audience, purpose, and genre. For example, use stories to teach reading to younger students, descriptions to explain to a sister class abroad about their town, and so on.

IV. *Drafting*

Drafting and planning are recursive. As students start drafting, they may decide they need to reorganize, read, and research more about the subject. A good practice is to begin drafting by writing for about 10 minutes without interrupting each other. The length of time can vary depending on the age of the learners. You can use this time to also write. Then walk around the room interacting with students. Allow students to consult among themselves. At this stage, students can use either language.

V. *Revision*

Revisions can be done in pairs, groups, or as a whole class. Students work on one persons' draft. The author reads aloud his or her piece and entertains comments and questions of the other students. Often at this point, the author notices things he or she wants to change. Model how to direct comments to the content and organization. The audience is there to offer suggestions and comment positively on the author's writing. You may want to go first to model the process, including suggestions for changes. It is very common for the author, while reading aloud, to make specific changes. The number of students that will get to read depends on the age and personality. Revision focuses on content and organization. Is the content accurate and complete? Does it make sense? Is it appropriate for the audience? Does it follow the organization that the particular genre requires? Demands on revision increase as the students become more experienced writers.

Once students are used to the process, you can have different groups working at different stages of the process. For example, while one group is working on the first draft, another group is revising their first draft, while a third is rewriting their initial draft. These groups *should not* be formed by ability. Move around to help, especially the students who are revising.

VI. *Editing*

Students produce several partially revised drafts that they keep in their folder and share with you. Periodically, have them choose one piece to develop further and edit to perfection to get published. Editing follows the same procedure as revision, but focuses on grammar, punctuation, and spelling. Many of these errors, however, get corrected while revising for meaning. Use students' errors as the source for needed lessons.

VII. *Publishing*

Students continue to work to produce a final draft for publication. Each student should decide when the final draft is ready. Stories can be collated into a book with covers, title, date, author and publisher. These books are featured in the classroom lending library. Other places for publication are newsletters, bulletin boards, or web pages. Letters are mailed out to real people, and so on.

Routines and structure get students in the habit of writing. For example, students can write one story or paper a week, or they can write for a minimum of 30 minutes each day. If students want to write more, they should not be stopped. Writing is developmental; both the ability to write and to revise will get better with more writing and revising. Therefore, one cannot expect the first final drafts to be perfect. (You need to make this point clear to parents and administrators.) Students should store all their drafts with the date, so that their development over time can be observed.

The Approach in Practice: High School Students Write for a Real Audience[10]

The Process Writing approach provided the students in Bryna's high school ESL class the opportunity to write for a real purpose and to a real audience (their fellow ESL classmates). Bryna decided to introduce Process Writing to her students, because she felt it would help the students become more independent in their writing. She also believed that because the Process Writing ap-

---

[10]This project was carried out by Bryna M. Leeder.

proach allows for individual pacing and flexibility, it would be advantageous in a classroom of students with mixed second-language abilities.

Bryna worked with eight of her more advanced ESL students in the production of a video highlighting a news event from the students' countries of origin, and in the development of a student manual to help recently arrived ESL students acclimate to their new school environment. Bryna chose those projects, because she felt that they would help her students focus on both audience and purpose of writing. She also felt it would increase their confidence in speaking English, because many of her students were uncomfortable when speaking in their mainstream classrooms.

The students chose the following topics for the video:

- Carnival in Bolivia
- Teenagers in Addis Ababa
- Problems in Macedonia
- Music and Women in India
- Russian Schools
- People's Treatment in Russia

Bryna began by working on the news program. She explained brainstorming and semantic mapping to the students. The students began by brainstorming ideas for the news magazine video. They engaged in a lively discussion about which topics should be considered for the project. Topics included sports, words in other languages, women's rights and music, politics, economics, education, and current events. The students decided on two formats for the news magazine: a report by one of the students, and an interview-style report where one of the students would be the "expert" on aspects of their country.

Students then began mapping out their ideas. It was a collaborative effort with students first working all together to model one brainstorming session, and then partnering up to help each other with their own topics. Bruno, a Brazilian, was having difficulty thinking of something to write about Brazil. Margarite told him how she had always been interested in Brazil's Carnival festival. Bruno liked the idea of explaining about Carnival, especially because he would not be attending it that year.

The whole class helped Bruno work on a semantic map explaining the Carnival. Students then continued working with partners to help each other finalize their own maps. Voula knew from the start that she wanted to write about the conflict between Greece and Skopje over possession of Macedonia. She was able to complete her semantic map assisted by a partner. For some students, the semantic mapping helped them hone ideas for their topic; for others it was a starting point for further research. At this point, the students were at different stages in their writing, but continued helping each other while working on their own projects.

The students then worked on writing their first drafts. Bryna discovered that this was a difficult process for some students. They had difficulty beginning the writing. She had assigned much of the first draft writing as homework assignments. Some students were able to complete their drafts at home and came to school ready to input their first draft into the computer. With the others who were having difficulty, Bryna suggested that they return to brainstorming their ideas to get a clearer picture of what they wanted to say. This seemed to help those students who were struggling. Aida had prepared some notes at home of information she wanted to include in her piece on students' leisure and social activities in Addis Adaba. Margarite helped her organize the notes in question form, which seemed to help Aida.

When the students had completed their first drafts, they shared them with the rest of the class. Students worked together to offer suggestions, question inconsistencies and misunderstandings, and confirm each other's impressions. They helped each other revise their pieces so that they became more personal and in-depth. Margarite also helped Nisha make her essay on Indian music more interesting by including information on the music teenagers in India listened to. It was suggested to Voula that her paper on Macedonia would be clearer if she provided the readers with a map highlighting the Macedonian sections of Greece and Skopje so that they would better understand the countries, territories, and their relations to each other. Following a suggestion from another student, Voula also included a description of her family's involvement in a rally in New York City protesting the fact that Skopje was using the name Macedonia.

The students revised their pieces both at school and at home. Voula decided to revise her information on the trouble between Greece and Skopje once she had discussed it with her mother and gotten more information about it. Nisha was able to give Nataliya help in revising her draft on Russian schools. Nataliya had written in her essay that there was "one big school for all the students." Nisha questioned her about that and Nataliya explained that what she was trying to say was that each school accommodated every grade. With Nisha's help, Nataliya revised the sentence so that it was better understood.

Much of the editing work done on the project was attended to once the work had been written on the computer. Nataliya, who had been at the school for a few years and had an understanding of the word processing program used by the school, showed the students how to use the spell check feature of the program. The editing portion of the writing process approach also proved to be a perfect time for Bryna to conduct ESL mini-lessons, because many of the editing corrections involved missing articles and incorrect vocabulary or prepositions.

When the students had finished their drafts for the videotaping reports, they worked with partners to help prepare their oral presentations. They highlighted the main ideas of their reports, so that they would not be so dependent on reading the text, and would be able to look into the camera while they presented their reports. By practicing aloud with a partner, the students saw the need for further editing to clarify main ideas, show sensitivity to an American audience, eliminate repetitive language, and improve endings. For example, in her draft Aida had written, "In Addis Adaba teenagers act different because it depends which school they go to." While she was practicing on tape, she realized that this sentence did not fully explain what she wanted to say, so she prefaced it by saying, "In Addis Adaba we have different schools like French, Indian, Armenian, and American."

Bryna used the same format for working on the student manual. They brainstormed together possible topics to include in the manual. Bryna organized their ideas on a semantic map. She then suggested that each student select a topic and write about it for 10 minutes to see whether this topic interested them. She found, however, that the students were not able to smoothly transition into working on their own at that point. She felt that the students might have needed more time to brainstorm and discuss the topics they had selected. Because class ended as the students were finishing their initial draft, Bryna suggested that they take what they had written home and either continue working on that topic, or select another topic about which to write.

Most of the students returned the next day with rough drafts on one of the topics. They read these aloud and got feedback from the other students on what they had written. It turned out that, even though Bryna had not assigned specific topics to the students, every student had selected a different topic from the semantic map. The final topics were:

* Getting in Trouble
* Procedures
* Guidance
* Feelings and Adjustments
* Academics
* ESL Class
* Sports

The students still worked better when collaborating with partners. A few students were having difficulty working on their topics, so the whole group worked together to give them some ideas. Progress for José was especially slow. He had a lot of problems coming up with ideas to write about, even with the help of the other students. He finally began to write about sports after the fifth day.

Nataliya had written about the problems ESL students might encounter with U.S. students who ignored them or teased them for not speaking English well. She had talked about strategies for ignoring such behavior. Samantat offered suggestions on how to make friends with Americans, such as getting involved in extracurricular activities, which Nataliya included in her piece.

Students also helped each other by suggesting where to research further information about their piece. For example, Jatinder suggested that Voula consult the student handbook to get more information about student infractions. Her suggestion was also followed by Taline, who found the information she needed to develop her topic further in the student handbook.

Bryna helped in the organization and revision of the content. Nisha had written a piece about the homework policy of the school, but had included a discussion about teachers. After Bryna had pointed out the two different topics to her, Nisha decided to separate her paper into two sections, one on homework and the other on teachers.

Some students needed more direction from Bryna than others. José was having difficulty elaborating on his writing. By asking pertinent questions, she was able to show José how to include more information in his story. For example, he had written: "If you play one of these sports, you have to go every day after school to practice." Bryna asked him how long the practices were. He then added "for four hours" to his sentence.

Being aware of their audience also helped students improve their writing. Natalilya had written, "You put your coat in a special place where all the students kept their coat." When she was revising, she changed "place" for the more specific explanation: "room that was locked and you could get your coat out only when school ended."

Most of the editing for these papers was also done on the computer. When the editing was done, Bryna had each student print a final draft of the essay, which was included in the student manual.

Bryna saw the value of the writing process and peer collaboration as a means of improving students' interest in learning and expressing ideas. She witnessed many lively and prolonged discussions about the topics written in the manual and for the videotape. She saw an increase in students' awareness of audience. The students knew they were writing for their peers, and were sure to include items and information relevant to them. Bryna reported that she no longer saw a passive group of students always waiting for her to lead the class, but rather, she saw a very proactive group of students ready to initiate discussions, express their opinions, and practice their oral English.

PROCESS WRITING: COMPUTERS

Purpose

Computers have become an important tool in the writing process. Revision is basic to good writing, and computers greatly facilitate that process. Students are more willing to revise when using a word processing program. Printed work looks neat. Even small children's writing has a book-like appearance. By responding to text written on the computer screen, teachers of second-language learners are able to correct and explain mistakes, or suggest alternative ways of writing something while the students are working on the piece. Students are able to immediately interact with the teacher to ensure complete understanding of what needs to be revised.[11]

1. Do prewriting and planning activities as recommended for Process Writing. If the class needs to go to a different room to use computers, do brainstorming, semantic mapping, and other prewriting activities on chart paper, which can then be taken to the computer room to be hung up.
2. Allow students to do their first draft either on the computer or with pencil and paper.
3. Walk around the room assisting students as needed. Let students assist each other.
4. For revisions and editing, follow the recommendations for Process Writing. You can work one to one sitting at a computer with a student, or students can work as partners helping each other, or a revising and editing circle can be set up in a corner of the room where groups of students take turns revising drafts with or without your assistance.
5. Print final products. Let students illustrate either by hand, or by using software programs that produce illustrations.

Tips for better utilization of the computers for Process Writing:

- Have students learn how to touch type.
- For very young children, draw a large keyboard with the capital letters and their corresponding small letter.
- As a reference for those frequently used software programs that are written only in English, it is helpful to write their basic directions on a poster board in the native language and hang it in the computer area.
- To motivate students, print their first product immediately, even if it is something they have dictated.

The Approach in Practice—Teacher's Responses to Bilingual Students' Writing: The Computer Changes the Process[12]

Charles is an ESL high school teacher who adapted his teaching style to incorporate the use of the computer in his writing classes. For 16 Vietnamese- and Spanish-speaking students from Grades 9 to 12, computers became an important element in their writing process.

---

[11]See Brisk (1985), Daiute (1985), and Forcier (1996), for further information about this approach.
[12]This project was carried out by Charles Skidmore.

The students, who were all in Charles' advanced ESL class, had a wide range of writing abilities. They met three times a week in the classroom and twice a week in the computer lab. There were 16 IBM computers and 2 printers in the lab. Students worked on the written piece both in the classroom and in the computer lab.

Topics for the writing assignments were introduced through readings and classroom discussions. Charles integrated the teaching of all aspects of language skills (i.e., reading, writing, speaking, and listening), to interesting topics. He also helped the students become familiar with American literature and themes of Western civilization by relating the ideas to the students' own cultural experiences. For example, Charles introduced the play *The Glass Menagerie* to the students by suggesting that its theme was escape. He then asked the students what escape meant to them. Students were then asked to write an autobiographical essay about escape. After having explored escape through their own experiences, the students read *The Glass Menagerie* and did a character analysis and wrote summaries of the plot. The unfamiliar literature of the new culture was introduced to the students by relating the topics to experiences that the students had had.

Issues and topics in Western civilization and American history were introduced in a similar fashion. The students' voices and experiences were expressed in the different genres of their writing.

Some students preferred to write a first draft by hand before working at the computers, whereas other students typed their drafts directly on the computer. Charles allowed for this flexibility. The students printed some of the drafts so that Charles could comment on them. However, Charles found that students understood his explanations better when he worked directly with them while they were writing at the computer. The final version was shared with the whole class.

Charles actively interacted with the students while they wrote on the computers. He answered questions, read aloud, asked probing questions, pointed out and discussed problems, or simply made a quick comment while walking by a student. Sometimes he focused on one problem or briefly answered questions; other times the interaction between him and the student required more time while together they revised or constructed a piece of writing.

These student–teacher interactions took place throughout every stage of the development of the written piece. The more insecure writers often checked before writing. Elizabeth was writing about the explorer Verrazano. Before writing, she called Charles:

E: What did he do?
C: He was sailing for France, even though he has an Italian name …
E: He was Italian, right?
C: Right, but he was sailing for France

E: What's his name?
C: Verrazano

Elizabeth, satisfied that she understood the basic information, went on to write that section of the paper.

Charles reviewed each stage of what most students wrote. Typically, he stopped by a student and read aloud what was on the computer screen. As he read, he pointed out problems and raised questions to help the student find a solution. After helping the student improve what was written so far, Charles gave some direction on how to continue. For example, Charles and Armando were reviewing what Armando had written about Laura, a character in *The Glass Menagerie*. Toward the end of the interaction Charles read aloud: " ... when Laura come to dinner ... "

C: Do you want the present tense there?
A: came (making the change)
C: came ... good! You're still not ready to end though, you still have to get the part that Laura falls in love and ends up being hurt by Jim. You can finish it up in a couple more sentences. Your basic ideas are there, but use the last 10 minutes to get the last idea, that this loving Jim, that being with him turns out to be very painful for her.

The students dictated the nature of the interaction. Werner usually liked to discuss completeness of content. Elizabeth, a less skillful writer, laboriously checked content, grammar, spelling, punctuation, and every detail of the piece. Charles sat by her side and they read together from the screen, stopping, discussing problems, and confirming every correction that she made.

Depending on the needs and the situation, Charles addressed the whole class, a group of students, or individuals. Normally, it was only at the beginning or end of the class period, and usually for general instruction purposes, that Charles spoke to the class as a whole. More than 90% of the interactions were done with individual students in response to specific language or content needs. With the beginning writers these interactions resembled the strategies used with young children developing language or second-language learners at the early stages of second-language development. Mercedes, an emergent writer, raised questions about Magellan while writing her research paper. Charles answered and carried on a long discussion to help her develop one sentence. (Underlining indicates the words that Mercedes decided to use in her final sentence.)

C: for Spain, right!
M: proved that the world was round

C: Explain to me a little bit more. How did he prove it, with a scientific experiment?

M: No

C: No, what did he do?

M: (unintelligible)

C: He and his crew ... actually he died before he finished ... but sailed ... they were the first ones to sail all the way around. So ... when you make a statement I want you to give me the next piece of information that proves it or shows how. So you can't just say he proved the world was round unless you tell me how. That's what these longer papers are about, a research paper, you are giving me that extra piece of information. I want something like <u>He and his crew</u>, you know crew?

M: yes

C: OK ... <u>were the first to sail</u>

M: sail around the world

C: completely around the world. OK add it in.
    (Mercedes wrote: "He and his crew were the first who sailed around the world for Spain.")

He helped Mercedes by asking probing questions, expanding her language, confirming her suggestions, and providing input that eventually became part of the student's own language. Bit by bit, whole sentences got constructed, using lots of the teacher's language.

Charles helped the students according to their needs. With Mercedes, he had to monitor the process of the initial writing. They made meaning together. With the more advanced students, he discussed the ideas and then left them to write on their own. When helping Armando, Charles raised the problem after reading aloud the text on the screen:

C: (Armando had written "she is shy") ... All right. You say the way she acts basically as a little girl, when you are telling this you can't just say she acts like it, you have to tell what it is that she does.

A: (unintelligible)

C: All right, so maybe that's where you want to go from there. What are the things that make her look like a little girl, what are her actions? (Charles started working with the next student.) Armando wrote "She like to play to recores and play with the Animal glasses." (She liked to play records and play with the glass animals.)

Although most interactions were with individual students, there were times when more than one student took part in a discussion. On one occasion, Charles was discussing how to start a new piece with Tuyet. The sentence they decided on also appeared on Son's screen. Son was sitting at the computer next to Tuyet and had paid careful attention to the discussion. On another occasion, when Charles was helping Son find the appropriate word, Marcial, José, and Tuyet, who shared the same table, joined in the discussion.

Through all the discussions Charles had with the students, the main focus was meaning. Even when discussing other aspects of language, such as text cohesion, a grammatical mistake, or spelling, he showed how it obscured the meaning of what was written. As Charles was reading Them's paper aloud, he pointed to the screen and said:

> C: I want a transition here. You've been talking about the Greeks. You can't just start all of a sudden "In Rome ... " You've got to tell me: As the Greek Empire faded ... or ended or stopped ... a new Empire arose, the new Roman Empire. Then you can tell this.

He not only told the student that he needed a transition, but discussed it in order to make sense from the whole text. At another time, as he was reading Tuyet's piece on the computer screen, Charles noticed that "reached" was missing the "ed." He said: reached ... past tense ... e, d, because it is past, it was a long time ago.

He read it as it was supposed to be, gave the grammatical explanation, spelled it, and also noted the semantic reason, attacking the problem from different linguistic levels.

With spelling problems, he often sounded out the word until the student figured out the correct spelling. However, besides focusing on sound–letter correspondence, Charles concluded with a brief semantic explanation. In that way, he tried to give students the message that the most important aspect of writing is to confer meaning.

Charles not only helped solve specific problems, but also enhanced the students' awareness of language, how it works, how text is organized, and the purpose of the pieces they were writing, thus developing the learners' metalinguistic awareness.

The responses to the students' work while writing on the computer were very different from the correction of writing done on paper. Traditionally, students write compositions that they hand in to the teacher to be corrected. The teacher then returns the corrected composition to the students, assuming that they read the comments written by the teacher. The teacher was the judge of the students' writing.

In the approach used by Charles, the relationship between teacher and student was more of an editor–writer, in which the teacher discussed problems with the students and together they reached a solution. Therefore, changes are negotiated rather than dictated by the teacher. These "negotiations" can be quite long, but because they are oral, they are quicker and less cumbersome than most written responses. Teachers spend between 20 and 40 minutes responding to each student's paper.[13] Charles, on the other hand, reached an average of 10 students in a 50-minute period. He was also able to use many other strategies not available in written responses, because of the ability to interact orally with the student.

The students often shared the printed drafts of their work with Charles. However, they often found the written comments ambiguous and requested clarification. Tomi called Charles because he had circled the word "widow" in the printed draft.

Tomi:	Amanda is a widow?
C:	She is not, because her husband is not
Tomi:	Not married
C:	They are married. What makes a woman a widow?
Tomi:	When a husband dies.
C:	All right, but he is not dead; he left, but he is not dead
Tomi:	So they are divorced.
C:	They are divorced. Exactly. So she is a divorcee (he spells it while Tomi types. Tomi types "divorced") No. The person is called divorcee
Tomi:	e,y?
C:	No, e, e.

Through this 10-turn interaction, actual teaching was taking place. Tomi learned the difference between "widow" and "divorcee," as well as "divorcee" and "divorced."

Often students reacted negatively to Charles' written comments, whereas they were more accepting of his oral remarks. For example, Charles had returned comments he had made on Elizabeth's first printed draft. It had many correcting marks, making the paper look messy. There was a note stating: "Elizabeth, you did a very good job!" Nevertheless, Elizabeth asked Charles if she should throw away that version and start anew. It took some convincing to make her realize that the corrections were all minor ones, easily fixed. In contrast, during a previous session, she and the teacher had thoroughly revised another piece directly on the computer screen. Elizabeth painstakingly worked at improving it, never suggesting that maybe she should clear the file and rewrite the paper.

The students also, in some instances, seemed to conference better when they did it at their computers. Charles came to them, and stood at their side, so the

---

[13]See Zamel (1985).

students, in a sense, were still in charge of their piece, making the teacher's role that of a helper. Conferencing at the computer seemed less intimidating for some students.

The conferencing that did take place was highly individualized and accommodated to the language of the learner. The students set the agenda for the interactions, which were directed to the language needs of the moment. They focused mostly on content; on helping students make meaning. Charles patiently continued the interaction until the students arrived at what they wanted to say. Charles was also able to expand on the language of the beginning English students. He modeled correct language forms and confirmed correct usage. There was much talk about language and writing while the pieces were being revised.

Charles has found that using the computer in his writing process classes has changed the way he teaches writing. Before using the computer, students usually did their writing at home. They handed in their papers to Charles, who commented in writing; then the students produced a second, and usually final, version. Through the use of computers, the students write in class, actively interact with both teacher and other students, and revise their papers as many times as they want or need to. In this process they learn much about English and writing.

The students' writing and revising strategies greatly improved. Their questions became more sophisticated They became more aware of reaching an audience with their writing and were more excited about publishing. They entered contests and submitted their work to school magazines and newspapers. Three students won honorable mention in a statewide essay contest. Charles had never entered students in the contest before. Using the computer as an integral part of the writing process converted the task of writing into a pleasurable activity for both Charles and his students.

SHOW NOT TELL

Purpose

The Show Not Tell approach helps increase students' use of detail and clarity in story writing. Students learn to clarify detail and draw a picture or scene with the words they write. For example, students write: "The movie was fantastic because it was so real." What is meant by "fantastic" and "real"? When working with bilingual students, the approach shows how students from different cultures picture something. Show Not Tell can be applied to writings the students produce through the use of other approaches.[14]

---

[14]See Caplan (1983) for further information about this approach.

Procedure

1. Practice for about 10 minutes daily having students expand a general statement into a paragraph. Examples:

   The room is vacant.

   Lunch period is too short.

   She has a good personality.

   Have students write so that the reader can *picture* what they mean. Share some of the pieces with the class each day. Read them aloud and have students comment only on the content of the writing.

2. Apply the approach to revision by having students work in groups. The "editors" underline sentences they think are underdeveloped or unclear. The writers then have to work to improve the sentence by expanding it and clarifying it. They then resubmit to the group for further comments or suggestions.

3. Daily writing can be used to improve specific techniques, such as persuasive argument—debating the pros and cons of a short lunch period; or comparison and contrast—showing similarities of school in native country and school in the United States; or sequencing—listing the steps for making a dish native to students' countries, and so forth.

The Approach in Practice—"She Was Dazzling": Making a Picture With Words[15]

It is often the experience for children learning a second language to be removed from their classroom for a certain time during the day or week to work with another teacher or assistant in a small group on various language skills, a program often referred to as a pull-out program. This was the case for the three children with whom Beth worked. They worked with an ESL teacher who saw the children twice a week for 45 minutes. Beth, a graduate student volunteer, was working with the ESL teacher to help improve the writing skills of the three fourth-grade students, two girls (Misha from Russia and Min from China) and a boy (Andre from Russia). All three students were considered advanced English learners, although Misha was a less advanced writer than the other two.

Beth's role was to support the ESL teacher in teaching Process Writing to the students. Students initiated writing with their ESL teacher, so Beth decided to work on teaching the students to add more detail to their stories. Beth felt that the Show Not Tell approach would help her accomplish this goal. Because she met with the students only once a week, she had to adapt the approach.

In their ESL classroom, the students had been studying fairy tales and were working on writing their own. Beth first reviewed their knowledge of the five

---

[15]This project was carried out by Elizabeth E. Morse.

senses and the importance of the who, what, when, where, why, and how questions in writing. She felt that the introduction of these two concepts would give the students a framework from which to work when adding details to stories they had written. Beth explained to the students that they should picture in their minds what the characters looked like and then write down a description. Initially, Andre had written a simple sentence about the setting and characters in his story:

> There was a castle and there was a king with his son. His son was a prince. He hated peas. The king hated peas too. King's name was Francis and the prince name was Christopher.

After working with the students on mentally picturing the characters and setting, Beth saw some improvement in the details of the descriptions. Andre revised his description of the castle to include that it was made of straw. When Min was having difficulty mentally visualizing her characters, Beth suggested that she draw a picture of them first, then write a description from the picture she had drawn. Min drew a picture of a king and queen and then described them: " ... She was pretty, She had brown hair and a betuflul smeles." And, " ... a wicked king he was ugly, and had red big eyes."

Beth taught the students to *show* attributes of their characters rather than just *tell* what they were like. She assisted students with difficult vocabulary. She helped them find words they needed or correct those they had attempted. While reviewing with Andre his story, Beth asked:

	How does the reader know that the king and prince were poor?
Andre:	They have those, you know, things in their clothes.
Beth:	What?
Andre:	You know. How do you say? (makes a circle with his hands)
Beth:	A hole?
Andre:	Yeah, a hole. How do you spell it?
Beth:	I'll write it here for you. What do you want to say?
Andre:	They wore clothes that was old and had holes.
Beth:	Okay.
	Beth then noticed the word *drizzeling* on Andre's paper
Beth:	What do you mean here?
Andre:	Um ... The princess was like shiney.
Beth:	Do you mean dazzeling?
Andre:	Yeah. That's it. How do you spell it?

Beth also tried to show the students the importance of adding more information in their stories by using the "wh" (who, what, when, where, why) framework. Andre had written a story about a king and a princess, who at the end of the story had died. He had not, however, given any explanation as to the princess' death. Beth reminded him that the readers might want to know why the character had died, so he added: " ... pea got alive, it got teeth too and the pea ate the princess and no one knew what happen."

Of the three students, Misha seemed to be having the most difficulty writing stories. She had moved from her native Russia to Israel when she was four years old. She had fond memories of Israel and talked about returning there when she was 16. There she learned to read and write Hebrew, which she liked learning. She did not show the same enthusiasm for English.

She was very reluctant to work in class and often balked about having to write, complaining that it hurt her hand. After two sessions of her leaving in tears and refusing to revise, Beth thought about having Misha use the computer instead of writing by hand. When Beth suggested this to Misha she was very excited. When Misha was living and going to school in Israel she used the computer frequently. It seemed to change her whole attitude about writing. While checking on her progress during one session, Beth thought that Misha had cut one of her stories and left out some important parts. When she questioned it, Misha explained that she was reorganizing her story so "that it sounds better." Misha was becoming more conscious of chronological order in her story.

Although the students clearly did increase the number of details in their story writing, Beth would like to have seen more growth and more carryover to their work in the ESL classroom. She saw the importance of close collaboration between tutors and classroom teachers in order to effect the best instruction for the students.

3

Approaches
With Focus on Reading

The approaches presented in this chapter provide a variety of ways to develop
and enhance reading ability. Teachers can combine them and adapt them to address different needs and age levels. The following approaches are described in
this chapter:

- Word Cards
- Shared Reading
- Vocabulary Connections
- Response to Literature Strategies
- Reader-Generated Questions

Word Cards and Shared Reading are effective approaches to initiate students
to literacy in their native or second language. Word Cards was primarily developed for children to learn the sound–letter correspondence using their own
words. It is also a good way to get to know the students and their interests. Often
students are introduced to the written language through flash cards with words
that come from a textbook, or prepared by teachers. Word Cards allow students
to learn through the words of their interest. It is a particularly useful approach
for students who are learning a different writing system.

Some teachers have adopted the idea of using students' words for other vocabulary activities. Paul, an English language arts teacher with a good number
of bilingual students in his class, used words suggested by his students for the
weekly vocabulary list. Another teacher used the students' words for her
weekly spelling tests.

Shared Reading has been associated with young children and big books. It
can be adapted for older students using overheads as a way to share a reading
passage. Shared Reading offers a good complement to activities based on stu-

dents' own language. It gives students the opportunity to internalize the rich language of experienced authors. It is extremely helpful for students learning a second language because the language is modeled and repeated for them before they try reading aloud by themselves.

There are many ways to teach vocabulary. The approach included in this chapter (Vocabulary Connections) is particularly sensitive to students' cultural backgrounds. Much clarification and cross-cultural explanations can be done during the discussions on how students associate the words to their lives. This approach can be used in combination with any other approach included in this handbook where there is need for vocabulary development.

Response to Literature Journals and Reader-Generated Questions are useful for students who have gone beyond initial literacy. Response Journals are particularly good for fiction and Reader-Generated Questions are helpful with expository reading. However, they can both be used with either genre. The Reader-Generated Questions approach requires time to implement because it has a number of steps. This approach teaches students the different steps of the reading process, fomenting good reading habits.

Other approaches that are particularly useful with bilingual learners are Reading Aloud, K-W-L, and Framework for Critical Literacy (see Appendix B). Reading Aloud with expression by the teacher facilitates comprehension of difficult text or text in a second language. K-W-L and Framework for Critical Literacy effectively elicit students' background knowledge and explicitly teach other aspects of the reading process.

WORD CARDS

Purpose

The Word Cards approach helps the students understand the sound–symbol connection of words. Words initiated by the students are used to learn decoding skills. For bilingual students, the use of Word Cards can also help increase and enhance vocabulary and language use in both the first and second language.[1]

Procedure

Following is the procedure for the Word Cards approach:

1. Prepare strips of strong cardboard or index cards. The younger the students, the bigger and stronger the cards should be.
2. Every day have each student give a word. Write it down on the card. As you write, sound the word out and let students watch as you write. Make sure the students are facing the card. If students are reluctant to

---

[1] See Ashton-Warner (1963) for further information about this approach.

give a word, write down words that would represent something close to them. (Talking to the student might bring out some ideas.)

3. Give the cards to the students. Let them read them aloud and on their own. (Have kindergarten students trace the letters with their fingers.)
4. Keep a file box in which to place the cards. You may write students' names in the corner of the cards to keep track of whose words are whose. (You can also let the students keep their cards in individual envelopes.) If students give words in both languages, put them in separate boxes, labeling the boxes by language.
5. Every day have students find their own words, sit with a classmate, and read their words to each other.
6. If students fail to remember how to read their own words, help them by sounding out the letters. (Although Ashton–Warner recommends discarding them, we have found that students get very upset if this is done.)
7. Once students have between 10 and 30 cards, use the cards for follow-up activities such as:
    a. Taking a few and checking to see if students remember them.
    b. Choosing one to elicit discussion of a topic by the whole class or a group. Have students write about it.
    c. Having the students write their word on a large piece of paper and make a drawing.
    d. Spreading cards on the floor, reading one word, and asking students to locate it.
    e. Using them for spelling tests.
    f. Having students put together a dictionary, organizing cards alphabetically, and keeping them handy as reference when they are writing.
    g. Creating games with the words.

The Approach in Practice:
Kindergarten Students Learn to Read Chinese[2]

Musetta used the Word Card approach to assist her Chinese bilingual kindergartners understand the word–symbol relationship in Chinese. Musetta found, in her work as a bilingual teaching assistant, that many of her students did not have experience with Chinese print. She wanted them to learn to read by using words that they had purposefully asked for and that were relevant to them.

Six children worked with Musetta three times a week. She began by having the students each give her a special word to write on an index card. In the beginning, there were some students who could not think of any word they wanted

---

[2]This project was carried out by Musetta Leung.

written down. When this happened, Musetta prompted them by asking questions about their family, the weather, food, and so forth, so that she could elicit some sort of response from the children. As the sessions continued, however, the children were usually able to supply their own words.

Musetta usually had each child stand by her and say the word that he or she wanted her to write on the index card. The children then traced the characters that Musetta had made to form their requested word. There were other times when Musetta simply had the children say the word while sitting with the rest of the group. Musetta then wrote the word while sounding it out. Although she was concerned that the children would not pay as much attention when she did the activity this way, Musetta found that the child who had offered the word to her always watched her as she wrote the word. The cards were stored in the students' individual cubbies. When the children returned the second day, they were very excited about retrieving their cards. Some of them had remembered their word and were able to say it. After each student had said the word, Musetta had them trace the word. One of the students, Edward, asked Musetta where to start tracing, so she guided his finger to the first character of the word. When working with the whole group, often the children seemed bored while waiting for each child to say the new word. Musetta suggested to the students that they draw a picture of their word while they were waiting for their turn.

The students were then asked for another word to add to their packet of words. When the students had trouble thinking of a word, Musetta asked what they had eaten for breakfast, which prompted such words as *ice, milk,* and *egg.*[3] There were occasions when there was no word in Chinese. For example, Dennis could not think of a word, so Musetta asked what he had eaten that morning. He replied, "cereal." Because there is no Chinese word for cereal, Musetta asked what he had with the cereal. When he offered the word *milk,* Musetta asked if he wanted that word added to his pack, Dennis agreed. Although the students did need help in thinking of words sometimes, Musetta found that the words elicited with her help were often the words that the children did not remember. Dennis, for example, did not remember the word *milk* the next day.

On one occasion, the children were asked to create sentences using their word cards. After modeling an example, Musetta asked the children to make their own sentences. Dennis, who is not usually quick to answer, was the first to offer a sentence. The other children also created phrases and sentences, such as: *four airplane, fall rain* (acceptable in Chinese), *five cookies, seven glasses of milk.* Musetta took all the phrases and sentences created by the children and made a book out of them. The children were very attentive when Musetta showed them the book. On each page she had written the phrases or sentences created by the children and had drawn a picture to go with the words. She

---

[3]All words were said and written in Chinese. We are using the English equivalent for convenience.

pointed to the words on each page while she read them to the children. The children then spontaneously repeated the sentences. The book was a great success. One of the children even took the book to his homeroom to show to his classmates and to his third-grade reading partner.

A few days later, the children enthusiastically read their book. They were able to read the words even without picture cues. They then played a game with the book and the word cards. While Musetta reread the book, each child raised his or her card into the air when he or she heard the word read by Musetta. After the children had learned more words, they were very eager to make another book. For this book, Musetta wrote the words on the top of the page, and the children illustrated each page. On the suggestion of one of the students, each child illustrated the page on which his or her own word had been written.

As the weeks progressed, and the children were used to the word card procedure, they developed a routine. When Musetta held up a card, the children first identified its owner. Then, the owner of the card, usually with a big smile on his face, said the word. Musetta praised them for their "super memory," to which the children smiled, or replied, "Of course!"

Musetta had made individual folders with two pockets into which she inserted the word cards of each child. On one pocket was a picture of a "happy face" into which the children inserted the words they knew; on the other pocket (with a sad face), the children placed the words they still did not know. The children were very happy to receive the folders, and became very possessive of them. They enjoyed taking out their word cards, studying them, and counting them to see how many they had accrued.

The use of word cards also helped to involve the children's parents. Fiona once approached Musetta and sadly told her that she had asked her mother to write the word *turtle* in Chinese for her, but her mother was unable to. Musetta suggested that she use that word on one of her new word cards. Fiona smiled at this suggestion. Fiona then asked Musetta to write the word *turtle* on another card so that she could bring it home to show to her mother. She did not want to use her own card for fear of losing it at home! Seron also asked if he could take home his folder and "teach" his father his words.

The children had a take-home book in which they wrote two of their favorite words. They drew pictures to go with the words they had written. The children took the books home and read the words to their parents.

Although some children were still having difficulty remembering their words, by the end of the word card project, Musetta found that many of the children were able to read all of their words as well as many of the other children's words. She notes that some of the difficulty the children had in remembering the words might, in part, be due to the problem of translating words from spoken Cantonese to written Chinese. For example, Seron had given the spoken form of the word *home*, which is different from the written form. Although Musetta explained this difference to Seron, he was still not able to remember the word when he saw it on his card. She was, however, confident in saying that the Word Card approach was effective for teaching beginning Chinese literacy skills.

SHARED READING

Purpose

This approach teaches reading through modeling and coaching using authentic literature, and introduces decoding strategies in context. Students are exposed to authentic literature in either their first or second language. They learn, through practice, the formal language of written text. This approach helps second language development by providing repetition, but in the enjoyable context of a story and through authentic language. It helps in developing confidence because learners internalize language patterns that they can apply to their own language use.[4]

Materials

Choose stories with repetitive patterns, songs, or poems. When working with a large group of young children, obtain or produce big books; when working with older students, transparencies can be used.

Procedure

Following are the procedures in the Shared Reading approach:

1. Read aloud a story from an original book. Students listen only.
2. Read the story from the big book or transparencies using a pointer to show where you are reading. Read with fluency and expression.
3. Allow students to join in if they want to. Repeat this procedure as many times as needed. Prepare response activities for students who do not need to continue to participate in the repetitive reading of the text. For example, students can write about their favorite character in the book, write a different ending for the story, and so on.
4. Let individual students read to the class also using the pointer.
5. Have small versions of the original available so that the students can borrow it to read on their own or in pairs. They can also borrow the books to take home.
6. Use the reading to do different types of exercises, such as the cloze procedure, looking for specific words, letters, etc.
7. Have students develop their own big books using an original story as a pattern.

---

[4]See Holdaway (1984) and Peregoy and Boyle (1996) for further information on this approach.

The same procedure can be used with a poem or song. It is best to write them on large chart paper so that the whole class can see.

Production of the Big Book

Students enjoy participating in the production of the big book. For students working in the second language, it provides added practice in reading and vocabulary recognition in that language.

1. Obtain 5 to 10 pieces of stock (32 x 42) or a large pad; felt pens (black, brown, and other colors).
2. Trace lines 1½ inches apart for the story line. Copy wording in the book exactly as the original in format and content. Leave space for margins and illustrations.
3. Copy or trace illustrations from the original (you don't need to do them all) or have students draw them on separate piece of paper, then paste it to the book.
4. Staple together or thread the pages through rings, including a title page.
5. Place on an easel for reading.

The Approach in Practice:
Bilingual Students Produce a Big Book[5]

The Shared Reading approach was selected by Peggy for the five Chinese bilingual students with whom she was working. Because Chinese is the main language spoken in these children's homes, Peggy felt that this approach would provide the students with the opportunity to enjoy stories in English and also increase their English reading skills.

Peggy worked with the classroom teacher to select an appropriate book to share with the children. They chose *Paper Crane* by Molly Bang, a book that they felt was especially appropriate for the children because the crane has a special meaning in the Chinese culture. (It represents longevity and is symbolic at birthday celebrations of Chinese elders.)

Peggy started the first session by placing a paper crane in front of the children. This sparked their interest and there were many questions about what it was, what were they going to do with it, could they have one, and so on. Peggy then talked to them about the crane and its meaning of longevity and good health in the Chinese culture. She explained to the children that cranes were a popular symbol at the birthdays of elders. One of the children remembered having seen a crane at her grandmother's birthday.

---

[5]This project was carried out by Peggy Yeh.

When the discussion of the crane and birthdays had ended, Peggy then read the title of the book and the author, and asked what they saw on the cover of the book. The cover showed a picture of a young boy holding a paper crane. This led to a discussion and many questions about birds. Although not directly related to the book, Peggy felt the discussion was important in order to elicit background knowledge from the children. She then continued by asking the children to predict what they thought the story was about. Edward believed the story had to do with "a little boy who gives his grandma a paper crane for her birthday." Another student predicted that it was a story about a boy who had lost a paper crane.

During the reading, Peggy modeled skills she wanted the children to use while reading. When she came to a word that she thought the children might not understand, she paused and asked them what they thought the word meant. For example, when she read the word *unusual,* she asked the children what it meant. One child replied, "It means something you do everyday." Peggy reminded the child that usual is something you do everyday, and then asked the children what happens when you "undo" something. Another child responded, "You don't do it," after which another student replied, "It's something you don't do everyday."

All through the reading of the story Peggy encouraged the children to make predictions about what would happen:

Peggy: Why do you think the stranger is back?
Tyrone: Maybe he's still hungry.
Peggy: Maybe ...
Feona: I know, I know, he wants the crane back!
Peggy: Hmmm, could be, let's read more to find out.

While reading, Peggy made sure that she used a different voice for the different characters in the story so that the children understood that there was meaning to what she was reading; that reading was not just decoding words. She was also careful to point to each word with a ruler as she read it. She felt that pointing with a ruler was especially important for the children, because directionality in reading Chinese (right to left and vertical) is quite different from English (left to right and horizontal).

When they had finished reading the entire book with Peggy, the children were invited to make their own big book version of the story. Peggy copied the text onto large paper. The students then illustrated each page. Peggy saw many opportunities for learning and skill building during these sessions. When the students weren't sure what to draw or had some questions about the drawing, she referred them back to the story to reread and discuss the section about which they had questions. They also practiced sequencing, decoding, and comprehension skills while they compiled their illustrated pages into a big book.

Because the pages had been mixed up during the drawing process, the students had to reread and put the pages in the correct sequence.

When the big book was completed, the children enthusiastically read and reread the book. For the first reading, Peggy had them all read together just for the practice of reading aloud. Peggy had the students work on their intonation in the second reading. The students read a third time, each taking turns going up to the easel to read a page. From the repeated readings, Peggy saw the students' confidence and fluency increase. One student in particular, who was usually quiet and not very vocal, read confidently and with a loud voice. Students were also able to remember many of the more difficult words because of the time they had spent discussing them during the readings.

Peggy found the implementation of the Shared Reading approach to be a valuable tool for the ESL students with whom she was working, and an effective approach to teach reading strategies to those students. She felt that her students had learned a great deal about story structure and had gained confidence in reading aloud.

VOCABULARY CONNECTIONS

Purpose

Vocabulary is the single most important area of second-language competency when learning content.[6] This approach to teaching vocabulary makes the students active learners and allows them to draw on their own cultural backgrounds and knowledge to establish meanings of words. Students make connections between the vocabulary and their own life's experiences before reading a selection, thereby validating their prior knowledge.[7]

Procedure

Following are the procedures for the Vocabulary Connections approach:

1. Choose a reading selection.
2. Choose 5 to 10 words crucial to understanding the selection, preferably in no more than one or two semantic fields.
3. Ask the students to look up the definitions of the words in the dictionary. (This can be done as homework.)
4. Have students discuss the definitions as well as give examples in their own lives of the selected words and their meanings. Clarify added meanings the words may have in the cultural context of the author.

---

[6]Saville-Troike (1984).
[7]See Torres-Guzman (1992) for further information about this approach.

5. Have students read the selection.
6. Have students retell or write a summary of the selection. Encourage them to use their new vocabulary.

The Approach in Practice:
Students' Background Knowledge in the Classroom[8]

For the seventh graders in Antolin's Spanish bilingual history class, the vocabulary approach helped the students relate words from their history text to their own lives. The 16 students in the class were from six different Latin American countries. The students had varying literacy abilities in their first language.

The students' history book was a Spanish translation of a book written in English specifically for students in the United States. Antolin felt that his students were at a disadvantage, because they might not be as familiar with U.S. history as what the authors of the text had assumed. He felt that the students needed extra support in understanding the vocabulary of the text, because the context of it in the history text might be incongruous to their experiences.

Before reading the chapter on the American Civil War (1861–1865), Antolin listed eight words that he felt were important for a true understanding of the chapter. The words selected were:

- alocución (address)
- abolicionista (abolitionist)
- guerra civil (civil war)
- emancipación (emancipation)
- plantación (plantation)
- proclamación (proclamation)
- estrategia (strategy)
- táctica (tactics)

The students first looked up the meaning of the words in the Spanish dictionary. The students worked in groups and wrote down the meaning of the words as one student read aloud from the dictionary. Students then discussed the meanings of the words until all were sure that they understood the meaning as explained in the dictionary.

Antolin then had the students try to find examples from their personal lives for which they could use one of the vocabulary words. The students willingly participated in the discussion. They related the terms to many aspects of their own lives from personal experiences in school to international politics. For the word *address*, one student used the example: "Principals address the whole school sometimes." Another student said, "Presidents do it all the time."

---

[8]This approach was carried out by Antolin Medina.

Many students were able to provide personal examples for civil war. A student from El Salvador, whose family owned land in the rural region of the country, related how his family had to leave their property and move to the city because they were "tired of being between two fires." He explained that his grandfather (the head of the family) had to supply food and other materials to both the government army and the guerrillas whenever they crossed his property. They were also constantly being warned not to help the other side of the conflict.

Although the students did understand the general meaning of *plantation* (i.e., a planted area farmed by paid workers), Antolin felt the need to explain its significance in the American Civil War period. After his explanation, students were able to relate it more easily to their experiences. One student saw a similarity between the plantations of that era and the situation of many Haitian laborers in the Dominican Republic.

When the students were not able to provide examples, Antolin explained the concept. When the students could not relate the term *abolitionist* to anything in their lives, Antolin explained how the abolitionists were opposed to slavery and were named so because they wanted to *abolish* it from in North America and the Caribbean Islands.

When the discussion of the vocabulary had finished, the class read the assigned chapter. Students took turns reading the selection. Following the reading, students answered general comprehension questions about the selection. For homework, the students wrote a summary of the major events of the civil war. In the summary, they had to include the vocabulary words that had been discussed prior to the reading.

Antolin noticed a great improvement in the summaries done by the students on this Civil War chapter. Previously, many students tended to copy sentences directly from the textbooks for their summaries. No student did that in their Civil War summaries. They showed an understanding of the main events of the Civil War and were able to use the vocabulary correctly.

Students in Antolin's class improved comprehension of their social studies text by learning relevant vocabulary. Internalizing new words required more than just looking up the dictionary definition. Students needed to associate the words with their personal experiences and background knowledge, to understand the cultural context of the words, and to discuss topics associated with these words.

RESPONSE TO LITERATURE

Purpose

The purpose of this approach is to have students think about what they have read, reflect on it, and relate it to personal experience and knowledge. It helps students better understand the text they are reading, while at the same time, making it personally meaningful to them. Bilingual learners are able to relate text to their unique experience as bilinguals. Students' background knowledge maps their interpretation of text. When reading text in a second language, students respond commensurate to their level of understanding. They have the opportunity to respond in their native language.[9]

Procedure

There are several ways to respond to literature. Following are three possible approaches:

Journals

1. Introduce the approach by modeling your own responses to a book the students have just read. Brainstorm with the students the kinds of things they could have written about. Use questions to help. For example: "How do you wish the story had ended?" "What did you think of the characters?" "What did you like and why?"
2. Give students a notebook.
3. Ask them to write their reactions to the book or chapters assigned, for example, one elementary school teacher told the students to write "letters" to her about their readings. Tell students not to write a summary of what they read, but write their personal reactions to the readings (i.e., feelings, ideas or questions).
4. Respond to the students' writings. Focus on what they are saying and on their questions. Do this activity twice a week, on days that you don't discuss the readings orally. It is important to schedule the activity so that you will have time to respond to each student's journal every time he or she writes. Therefore, do not schedule the activity with more frequency than you can respond.

Double-Entry Journals

This approach is similar to the previous one, but instead of reacting to the whole text in general, students react to selected sections. They copy parts of the book that they like on the left-hand side of the notebook and write their own reactions to that section on the right-hand side.

Point-of-View Pieces

Students write something as if they were actually involved in the book. For example, they can write a letter as if one of the characters had written it; with an-

---

[9]Peregoy and Boyle (1996) and Peterson and Eeds (1990) for further information about this approach.

other student, each taking the role of one character and writing a dialogue; they can write a diary entry, a speech, or have a phone conversation as if they were one of the characters; and so forth.

The Approach in Practice:
Response Journals in a Bilingual Classroom[10]

Angela implemented the Response to Literature Journals approach with her class of fifth-grade Spanish bilingual students as part of the English literature curriculum. She hoped that by using the method the students would become more actively engaged in English reading activities, and would be encouraged to share their own viewpoints and interpretations of the texts.

Angela started the method in conjunction with a unit on folk tales. During a 10-week period the students read and studied nine books:

- *The Giving Tree*
- *Why Mosquitoes Buzz in People's Ears*
- *The Legend of the Indian Paintbrush*
- *The Legend of Scarface*
- *The Weeping Woman/La Llorona*
- *The Village of the Round and Square Houses*
- *The Luminous Pearl*
- *Mufaro's Beautiful Daughters*
- *The Legend of the Food Mountain*

She began by reading the book *The Giving Tree* by Shel Silverstein to the class. She then shared thoughts, impressions, and questions about the book to the entire class, writing her impressions on an overhead projector as she thought aloud: "I enjoyed the special relationship shared by the boy and the tree. They loved each other very much. I noticed the different stages of the boy's life in which he would ask the tree for something. I wondered why the tree never said no." She then invited students to share their thoughts about the story while she wrote them on the overhead. Carla asked, "Why weren't there any other people in the story?" Jorge suggested, "What you do if you were in that situation?" Another student asked, "How about what we learn from the book? Like a *moraleja* [the moral]."

Angela also modeled how to relate the story to one's own life. She told the students that the tree in the book reminded her of her mother, and how her mother, like the tree, gives because it makes her happy. The children immediately understood the connection Angela was trying to make.

After the entire class had formulated questions together, Angela broke the students into groups to collaborate on additional questions to add to the list.

---

[10]This project was carried out by Angela Burgos.

She felt that in this way, students who were too shy to speak during the whole class discussion would have an opportunity to share in a smaller, less intimidating group. When the activity was done, Angela compiled a list of open-ended questions from those suggested by the students:

- What do you learn from reading the book?
- Why did the author write the book?
- Did you like or dislike the story?
- How do you feel about the story?
- If you could change anything about the story, what would you change and why?
- What would you do if faced with the same situation?
- How do you feel about the characters?

She explained to them that many of the questions could be used with any story and would help them in their response to literature assignments. Nevertheless, she encouraged the students to respond in whatever ways they wished.

The students were then given a notebook and asked to write to Angela about their reflections on *The Giving Tree*. Angela stressed the importance of writing personal reactions to the story and not a summary of what was read. She also emphasized that they should be more concerned about what they wrote than how they spelled what they wrote. They were able to write in either English or Spanish.

Initially, Angela noted that the students' responses were brief, but they did write about their personal reactions to the story. For example, Carla wrote in response to *The Giving Tree:* "the tree churent give so much to the boy because they boy is greaty." (The tree shouldn't give so much to the boy because the boy is greedy.) For the next lesson, Angela introduced the African tale *Why Mosquitoes Buzz in People's Ears*. Again, Angela modeled how to make connections between what happened in the story to one's own life. She related how when she was young she had told a lie and gotten her brother in trouble. The students understood the connection and wrote about similar experiences in their lives. For example, Susana wrote:

Dear Ms. Burgos,
The day I got in trouble was wen I was in quindergarden that a teacher tease my had and I BAit the teacher and skeeam and Rand to my mother and she say That y Bait her hand and she drent twish my hand. so then I had to brenger to th hospital.
(The day I got in trouble was when I was in kindergarten. That a teacher squeezed my hand and I bit the teacher. I screamed and ran to my mother and she said that I bit her hand and she didn't twist my hand. So then she said that I had to bring her to the hospital.)

In her response to Susana's entry Angela again makes a connection to the story:

Dear Susana,
I could understand why you got in trouble. Your mother didn't know the teacher
had twisted your hand. Now you know how the animals felt.

Several different activities were used throughout the 10 weeks to present the
various books. For several of the books, *Why Mosquitoes Buzz in People's
Ears, The Weeping Woman/La Llorona,* and *Mufaro's Beautiful Daughters,*
Angela conducted a whole-class guided-reading activity. She began by reading
the title and author, showing the cover of the book, and then asking the students
to predict what the plot of the story might be. The students made predictions
based on what they saw on the cover of the book. After a discussion of possible
plots and characters, in which all answers were accepted, Angela read part of
the story aloud while the students followed along in their own copies of the
book. She paused while reading to ask for more predictions as the story developed. After reading the story, the students responded in their journals.

The students also read one of the books independently. Angela gave them a
choice of one of three books, *The Legend of the Paintbrush, The Legend of
Scarface,* or *The Legend of the Food Mountain,* to read by themselves. She provided a brief description of each of the books so that the students would make a
better decision about which book to select. The students were allowed to either
read alone, or with other students. Angela provided index cards for the students
to write down any words they did not understand.

At first most students sat with one or two others discussing the cover of the
book they were reading, or looking at the illustrations in the book. When the
students did begin to read their books, however, many did so alone. When the
students had finished reading their books, they responded in their journals.

The students wrote in their journals, to which Angela responded, twice a
week. Although, initially their entries were brief, the students were able to relate what they had read to something meaningful for them. As they continued
reading the folk tales and responding to them in the journals, the students' responses were more detailed and they referred more often to the events and vocabulary of the text.

Mini-lessons were also conducted from time to time to help the students understand the process of the approach. Angela sometimes modeled a response to
the book they had read. At other times, she copied a response from one of the students to use as a model and shared with the whole class using the overhead projector. Carla had made an analogy between the character in *The Legend of the
Indian Paintbrush* and the mosquito in *Why Mosquitoes Buzz in People's Ears:*

Dear Teacher,
I really like the story because it says a lot of the things that happened and I feel
very good for him because its really good idea you now smashing to make some
paint. I think that his favorite thing is do is paint like the mosquito he like to bugg
on people's ears so the man like to paint and the mosquito like to bugg can you see
the diffents.

For some of the folk tales, Angela showed a video version. The students were then able to compare and contrast aspects of the book with what was presented on the film.

Angela found the journals to be a valuable resource for helping the more introverted students. Carmen was a student who rarely participated in class discussions. Angela saw growth in Carmen's confidence and abilities to relate to literature through her passages in the journal. She also used the journal for clarification and to ask further questions about the stories read. As an additional resource for evaluating the literacy development of the students, Angela used a Response to Literature Checklist.[11]

The Response Journals approach was an important component of the reading program for these students because it allowed the students to respond at their own reading and writing ability without fear of peer judgment or criticism. It also helped both Angela and the students keep pace with students' individual learning. The students were able to express themselves.

READER-GENERATED QUESTIONS

Purpose

The purpose of this strategy is to facilitate reading comprehension and foster recall by walking students through the steps of the reading process: stimulating background knowledge, predicting, actual reading, and synthesizing. The activities preceding the actual reading also provide an opportunity to teach vocabulary, teach how to produce questions, relate the topic to students' personal experiences, learn about students' background knowledge on the topic, and clarify possible contradictions with the author's intended meaning when students' and author's cultures contrast.[12]

Procedure

This activity has six different steps. When the text is in the students' second language, the native language can be used for the first three steps. Throughout the steps you should teach vocabulary, text structure, and other language skills that will facilitate the process of understanding this particular selection. Steps in this activity include:

1. *Stimuli.* Introduce the topic of reading through:
   a. pictures, graphs, maps, time lines;
   b. semantic map;
   c. real objects;

---

[11]See Peterson and Eeds (1990).
[12]See Henry (1984) for further information about this approach.

      d. title of the reading (and initial sentence); or

      e. statement of the general theme.

    During this step, explore the students' background knowledge on the topic, relate it to their own experiences, and clarify any misconceptions.

  2. *Generation of Questions.* Ask the students to generate from one to ten questions (depending on ability) about this topic. This can be done in several different ways:

      a. Write questions on the board or chart paper as students suggest them. (Put the name of the author by the question.)

      b. Let students generate and write down questions in small groups.

      c. Let students write questions individually.

  3. *Responding to Questions.* Have students guess responses to the questions. Depending on the size and level of the class, do it as a whole class or small group activity. Different groups can work on different questions.

  4. *Presentation of the Text.* Depending on the age and level of students and text difficulty, present the text by:

      a. Telling the story or content of the text to the students.

      b. Reading aloud the text.

      c. Letting the students read the text individually or in groups, either in class or as homework.

  5. *Checking Out Responses.* Ask the students to check the accuracy of their responses.

  6. *Final Activity.* Have the students write a summary, prepare a graph, outline the content, draw a picture, or some other activity that will help synthesize the content gained on the subject.

Follow-Up

If some of the questions the students asked were not answered by that particular text, take the students to the library or bring resources to the room, so that individually or in groups the students can look for responses. Another possibility is to have students interview experts to find out the responses.

The Approach in Practice:
Sixth Graders Cope With Science Texts[13]

For many second-language learners, content area study is a very complex, and often frustrating, process. Renate felt that the Reader-Generated Questions approach would be helpful to bilingual students studying science. Renate worked with four sixth-grade Spanish–English bilingual students enrolled in an inte-

---

[13]This project was carried out by Renate Weber Riggs.

grated Spanish–English bilingual program at an urban elementary school. Spanish was the first language of all four students, although three of the four students indicated that they preferred reading and writing in English to reading and writing in Spanish.

Renate decided to use this approach because she felt that the students would benefit from the cooperative learning atmosphere this approach incorporated. It would also be an opportunity for the students to use language for meaningful purposes. She followed a six-step plan for the five topics that she (with input from the classroom teacher) had wanted to introduce to the students. The topics were: Green Plants, Plant–Animal Cycle, Fungi (Mushrooms), Fungi (Molds), and Skeletal System.

In her introduction of the approach, Renate explained to the students that they were the ones who would be asking the questions about the specific topic, and that afterwards, they would investigate and research answers to those questions in the texts read during the classes. She felt it was important to show the students that they already had some knowledge about the topics. Renate encouraged group work and the use of Spanish in the students' discussions, even though she herself did not speak Spanish. She made every effort to help the students realize that their first language was a valid, viable, and important means of communication. Renate also functioned as the scribe during the sessions. She felt that writing for the students created a less stressful situation for them and facilitated the flow of the discussion.

The Study of Green Plants

The first topic introduced to the students was green plants. A semantic map was used to organize information students already knew about green plants. The students were given books with photographs and sentences to help stimulate ideas and formulate questions about green plants. Renate wrote the words "green plants" in the middle of a 9 x 12 paper and asked the students to say as many words as they could related to the subject of green plants. As Renate wrote the words on her paper, the students copied the words on their own papers. After there were a number of words on the paper, Renate explained to the students that they would categorize the words. She pointed to words such as *trunk, fruit, roots, stem,* and *leaves,* and asked the students what could be said about those words. One student replied: "It is a tree." Renate wrote *Parts of a Plant.* She then pointed out *soil, water, sun,* and the students correctly responded "need to grow." She continued categorizing the words until the students eventually understood the idea and began volunteering words from the map to fit into categories.

During her next session with the students, Renate explained to them that they would come up with questions that they wanted to learn about green plants. She began by writing two sentences on the board that the students were to copy on their papers: Green plants make their own food. All living things depend on plants. She then had George read the sentences aloud, and then explained that they would use those two ideas to help stimulate ideas for questions they might have.

Angel began by asking the question: "Why do trees have brown trunks and when they little the stem is green?" Renate was writing down Angel's question as he said it. With a little coaxing from her, Angel added the word *are* and corrected his question to " … when they are little the stem is green." Renate wrote the question on chart paper, and then had Angel reread it and write his name next to it. Other students contributed to the list of questions, following the same routine of dictating to Renate, rereading their question, and writing their name next to their question. The students copied the questions on their own paper. This was a perfect opportunity for Renate to see how they were writing their questions on the paper. She noticed that many had forgotten the question marks at the end of the sentence. When she asked what was needed at the end of all questions, everyone yelled, "Question marks."

When the students had generated six questions, Renate told them that they would now try to answer the questions to the best of their knowledge. The students enthusiastically began responding to the questions. Renate wrote down all their answers. She had forgotten to tell the students to leave a space between each question in order to write the specific answers related to that question later on, so the students had to write the answers below all of the questions.

When all the questions had been answered by the students, they opened their science textbooks. Renate read two paragraphs from the text and explained to the students that they were reading the book to find any answers to their questions. Renate used this approach as reading to learn, rather than reading to comprehend a story. Students, therefore, used several sources, in addition to the class text, to read about the topic.

Jorge found that two of the questions were answered by the text. Renate asked him to read the question first: "Why are plants green?" Jorge then referred to the textbook and read the answer: "Plants use chlorophyll to make their own food." As Renate was reading this answer to write on the chart paper, Jorge realized that that did not fully answer the question, and added: "Chlorophyll makes these cells look green."

Strategies Used for the Different Steps

Renate used different strategies for each step depending on the topic. For the first step, Renate used semantic maps to stimulate ideas for the green plant and skeletal system topics. Pictures and photographs from both science textbooks, as well as other books, were used when working on the plant–animal cycle and fungi–mushrooms topics. When the students were studying about fungi and mold, Renate brought in moldy cheeses, breads, and even a bottle labeled penicillin.

To produce questions for the plant–animal cycle topic, students looked at a drawing from a book about photosynthesis. The students worked in groups to discuss the drawing and come up with questions. Students discussed in their groups in both English and Spanish. After a few minutes, Renate called the groups together and wrote down the questions they had formulated.

Responding to questions was the third step in the process. The students used the resources available to them to find the answers to their questions. The students dictated the answers to Renate, who wrote them. On one occasion, as Renate was writing down what one student had said, he, Albin, noticed he had made a mistake and self-corrected. Albin had said, "Because when the animals breathe out oxygen, um, the plants breathe in carbon dioxide in." As Renate was writing his response on the chart paper, Albin realized his error and corrected himself: "Because when the animals breathe out carbon dioxide and the trees breathe in carbon dioxide."

The fourth and fifth steps in the process allow the students to verify the responses they made to their questions by investigating text books and other sources for their information. For example, on the lesson *Fungi/Mushroom,* Renate read about fungi from a biology book. The students then read through the passage again looking for answers to the questions they had generated. One of the questions the students wanted answered on this topic was, "Why is the bread blue?" George responded, after looking in the book, "Because it says–They send threads (pronounced threeds) of mold into the bread. Maybe that's not the answer." Renate explained to George that he had given part of the answer and that it could be added to the answer they were formulating for the question.

Renate stressed the importance of the format of the texts used. Texts with subheadings helped the students focus more quickly on what they were reading and where possible answers to their questions might be. As the students were looking through the books to find the answers to their questions, they were also learning the formats. For example, when reading the passage on the skeletal system, "The skeletal system functions in four ways," the students found a chart on the page explaining the four ways.

Renate also found it was important to ask students to explain their answers further if they did not seem to make sense. In one instance, one of the students answered the question, "Why does that have something black?" (the fungi topic), with "Because it doesn't work." Instead of asking for an explanation of the response, Renate simply wrote what the student had said. She later discovered, while speaking to a Spanish-speaking teacher, that the student had translated the Spanish phrase "no sirve" (it's no good).

To complete the cycle of the Reader-Generated Questions, various activities were implemented in order to review and insure an understanding of the topic. At times verbal review of the material was conducted, or other teachers asked questions about the topics. For the topic of fungi/mold, the student were asked to draw pictures of what a mold looked like. Some students also wrote captions under their drawings. For that particular session, students from a mainstream class had joined Renate's group. Michelle, one of the more shy students in the bilingual group, was able to discuss and explain the concept of molds to the students from the mainstream class.

Renate believes that Reader-Generated Questions is an excellent approach for development of academic language and recall of content material. She found that the quality and quantity of the students' questions improved during the activity. As the weeks progressed and the students were more involved in the activity, they began to realize that they could ask different types of questions and that there may be more than one answer to their questions. Renate also saw an improvement in how the students focused on the text when looking for answers to their questions. The students who participated in this activity recalled better than the rest of the class the topics covered in the science curriculum.

4

Approaches
With Choice of Focus

Some approaches are very flexible and allow teachers to use them to develop one or more aspects of literacy. Such approaches include:

* Graphic Organizers
* Language Experience Approach (LEA)
* Student-Directed Sharing Time and Group Discussion
* Cooperative Learning Strategies
* Cross-Age Project
* Critical Autobiographies

Graphic Organizers and the LEA are particularly useful with young students or second-language beginners. Graphic Organizers require thinking and discussion that can be done either in preparation to read or write or after reading or writing. Using Graphic Organizers before reading helps students explore their background knowledge, develop relevant vocabulary, and make predictions. Graphic Organizers are helpful to plan writing by organizing thoughts, establishing knowledge and gaps, and rehearsing the language. After reading, students can synthesize the content of the readings using Graphic Organizers. It helps with checking comprehension and fostering recall. This approach can help with clarity of ideas and organization when revising drafts. Graphic Organizers are very useful when working in a second language, because they display ideas concretely using a limited number of words. Even beginners can participate by offering just one idea.

The LEA was developed to initiate children to reading. We have used it with students of all ages to introduce the first and second language for both reading, writing, and language development in general. It is particularly helpful to introduce literacy in the native language to older students with limited or no schooling.

Student-Directed Sharing Time or Group Discussions are done completely orally, but enhance literacy development because they require students to discuss and think around a topic. These approaches can be easily integrated with reading and writing activities. It is easier for students to carry out this activity in their stronger language or bilingually. The nature of the activity changes with the age of the students. Younger children discuss spontaneously in relation to things that have happened to them, need more rules of behavior, and the leader is chosen as the activity starts. Older students can relate the discussion to issues in the curriculum, can do research in preparation for the discussion, and the leader can be assigned ahead of time.

Jigsaw is one of a great number of cooperative learning strategies. It can be easily adapted to develop one or several literacy skills for students of different grade levels and literacy abilities. The nature of the materials and the task dictate the level of difficulty. A science teacher efficiently covered her unit on human organs using Jigsaw. She provided extensive materials in the native and second languages of the students according to availability and quality. Students had to read, write, and create visual props to support their oral explanations of what they had learned about the organs. A foreign language teacher used simple directions for a game as reading material for beginners. The students focused on reading and playing the game to demonstrate comprehension.

Cross-Age Projects are appropriate for developing many literacy skills. Because older students practice skills in order to teach them to younger students, it is an ideal approach to remediate skills for upper grade students. The older students master material below their grade level, but they do not feel humiliated because they are preparing to be teachers. Thus, the content is below grade level, but the process is challenging. These projects have been used for literacy in general, reading, writing, math, and even to redevelop the native language of students who, by high school, had mostly lost it. The most crucial aspect of this approach is to give the older students the chance to prepare well before they start working with the younger students.

The Critical Autobiographies is a more complex approach that gives students practice in academic oral language, reading, and writing, while using a number of the other approaches recommended in this handbook. Most teachers have used this approach to fulfill interdisciplinary requirements. Students do not write a traditional autobiography, but write about the issues that are affecting them as bilingual–bicultural individuals. Teachers have used Critical Autobiographies from first through twelfth grade. Some teachers have paired to implement this approach. For example, a mainstream social studies teacher worked in coordination with an ESL teacher to implement units of the social studies curriculum and develop language and literacy to a combined group of English-speaking and bilingual students of different language backgrounds.

This approach helps teachers familiarize themselves with the situational factors that affect bilinguals.[1]

GRAPHIC ORGANIZERS: SEMANTIC MAPPING

Purpose

Graphic Organizers help students arrange information by utilizing the most important aspects and concepts of a topic into a visual representation. In addition to Semantic Mapping, described in this section, there are many other types of Graphic Organizers, such as Venn Diagrams, story maps, main idea–supporting details, and sense matrices (see Appendix C). Semantic Mapping stimulates vocabulary development and activates background knowledge. The maps display words, ideas, or concepts in categories and show how words relate to each other. Mapping helps students to visually organize information and can be an alternative to note taking and outlining. It is a very helpful prereading–prewriting practice. The organizers can also be beneficial as a postreading activity through which the students demonstrate and increase their comprehension of a topic.

For bilingual and second-language learners they are a tool for scaffolding knowledge and increasing vocabulary.[2]

Procedure

Follow these steps to execute Semantic Mapping:

1. Brainstorm a topic with the students. Write the topic on the board or on paper and have students write it on their paper as well.
2. Brainstorm other words related to the topic. These become the secondary categories written around the central theme or topic. Connect them with lines to the topic. The students write them on their papers.
3. Be creative: use words, pictures, phrases, geometric shapes, or colors to portray the map. Once the students have the idea, they can create maps in a variety of ways.
4. Discuss the ideas generated on the map. Ask, "What do these ideas have in common? How do they relate to each other?"
5. As the students answer these questions, group the words into categories; the groups can be labeled.

This activity can be done before reading a selection or in preparation to write about a topic. It can also be used after reading to check on comprehension or af-

---

[1]For a complete analysis of situational factors see Brisk (1998a, chap. 2).
[2]See Buckley and Boyle (1981), Homza (1996), Flood and Lapp (1988), Peregoy and Boyle (1996), and Perez and Torres-Guzman (1996) for further information on this approach.

ter writing to improve organization and completeness of a topic. Figure 4.1 is an example of a semantic map.

The Approach in Practice: Mapping it Out for Reading[3]

Semantic Mapping proved to be a successful approach for the three second-language learners with whom Judy was working. Judy worked with three siblings (a sister and two brothers) from Chile as a tutor. The children's parents had requested that Judy help the children with their homework, but after a few initial sessions, Judy felt that she would be more helpful to the children by increasing their English proficiency. The oldest child, Nancy, was 10 years old, the brothers were Pedro, 9 years old, and David, 5. She worked with the stu-

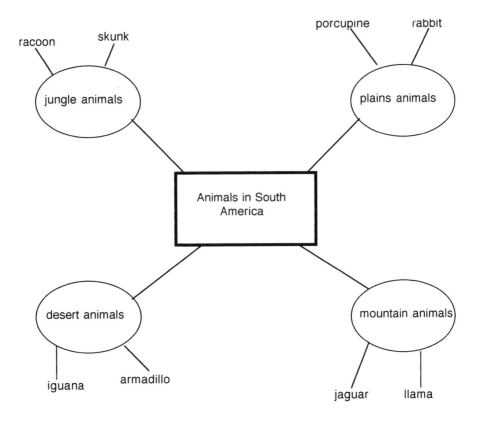

FIG. 4.1.   A semantic map.

---

[3]This project was carried out by Judy Casulli.

dents two days a week in their home after school. Although David was quite young and only beginning to read and write, he was able to actively participate in the lessons. In the beginning he volunteered words and then usually just drew pictures or circles when needed, but by the end of the sessions he was able to write some words, and copy others.

Judy decided to work with semantic maps because she felt it would help increase the vocabulary of the children. She also believed that using semantic maps was an effective way to stimulate conversation about a particular topic and was a good prereading and prewriting activity. The Semantic Mapping lessons were precursors to reading books and writing stories with the children.

Judy usually asked the children beforehand which topic they wanted to discuss during their next session together. In that way, she was able to find resource materials and books related to the topic in which the children were interested. The first topic chosen by the children was Halloween. The children had been in the United States for less than a year, so this was to be their first Halloween. Judy asked the children in English what they knew about Halloween. They replied in one word answers such as *pumpkin, skeleton*, and *witch*. Judy wrote down the words on chart paper as the children said them, and they copied the words into a notebook. Some of the words were said in English, and others were stated in Spanish. When a word was said in Spanish, Judy told the children what the word was in English and then proceeded to write it in English on the chart paper. If it seemed as if the children did not understand the concept of a word, Judy first tried to explain the idea in English, and then explained in Spanish when necessary. Once a good list of words was generated, Judy and the children discussed the more unusual ones. By discussing some of the words in a little more detail, Judy was able to see exactly what the children understood of the concept, and the children were able to practice more English.

When the discussion of the words had ended, Judy put up a clean piece of chart paper with the word *Halloween* in the center. She asked the children to think of how the list of words could be grouped into categories. The children understood what Judy wanted, and Pedro noticed that many of the words were names for animals. Pedro wrote the word *animals* to the lower left of "Halloween" and the children took turns calling out words that belonged to that category. When all the animal words had been written, David, the younger brother, drew circles around each word. The activity continued until all words had been placed in one of the four categories: Animals, Monsters, Pumpkins, and Trick or Treat. The discussion that took place during this activity was done in both English and Spanish with the children usually saying the key word in English, but explaining their reasoning in Spanish. Pedro tried to form simple sentences in English with the key word. Nancy did not want to say much in English. Judy followed this activity by reading a story about Halloween, *Rotten Ralph's Trick or Treat*. If a word from their map appeared in the story, Judy asked a question to further reinforce their new vocabulary.

The children had picked the topic of work for the second time they did Semantic Mapping. Judy began by asking the children to tell her some words that had to do with work. Nancy replied in Spanish *secretaria* (secretary). Pedro then offered the word *teacher*. Nancy objected because she wanted to continue thinking of other categories beside the specific name of a worker, for example, the place they work, the job they do, and so on. Judy tried to explain that the idea was to just write down whatever came to mind, and that they would organize it later. However, Nancy was quite adamant about organizing as they went, so Judy conceded. The children were able to skip the initial step of listing and worked right away at organizing their words into categories, because they had a good grasp of the concept. One problem with this particular mapping session was that the topic was too broad, which caused some confusion for the children. They ended up with a somewhat organized listing of words. They then worked on organizing the map by workers, under which was identified the place they worked and what they did at work. Again, after the session, Judy read a book to the children about people working. Figure 4.2 shows the final map on work.

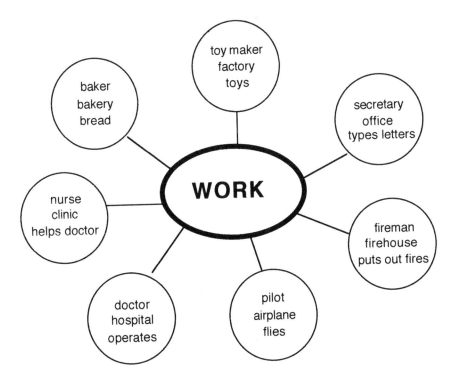

FIG. 4.2. The final map on work.

On one occasion the children had told Judy that for their next topic they wanted to discuss *airplanes*. However, Judy was unable to find a book suitable to discuss with the students, so she changed the topic to *food*. Although the students did participate, she found that they were not as attentive as usual and she had to coax words out of them. She realized that they were not as interested in the topic because they had not selected it. The children seemed to be losing interest, so Judy came up with the idea of making a Semantic Map of the food words by mapping out a grocery store. The children then enthusiastically began categorizing the words. In the end, their supermarket map contained the following sections: *fruit, vegetables, school supplies, toys, meat, dairy, frozen*, and *cereal*.

Judy tried to tie the lessons she was giving the children at home to what they were studying in school. Nancy told Judy that she was studying geography, so during one of the sessions the children worked on geographic terms. By that time, the children had definitely established quite an efficient routine for working on the maps. They began by directly organizing the words into categories. Pedro preferred providing the ideas and letting Nancy make the map. David was also becoming more involved in all aspects of the process. The children were able to categorize words into countries, mountains, canals, volcanoes, oceans, and capitals. As a follow-up reading activity to this session, the children looked at an atlas. The atlas provoked a lot of discussion. Nancy became very excited when they turned to a map of Chile. She spoke excitedly in Spanish about the map, and even emphatically refused to speak in English when it was suggested.

The last semantic map done with the children involved words dealing with the seasons after which they read the book *Chicken Soup with Rice* by Maurice Sendak. David asked to read for the first time. He usually just listened to his brother and sister read and then made comments. This time, however, he wanted to actively participate in the reading. Judy read a line and he repeated it. He was quite excited that he was "reading." Although clearly still at a preliterate stage, Judy noticed over time that David did recognize certain words that they had used during the mapping activities, and was able to write some of the words they had learned.

While Judy believed that the Semantic Mapping exercises done by her tutees helped increase vocabulary and conversation in English, she came to realize that Semantic Mapping could be used for many pre- and postreading activities.

LANGUAGE EXPERIENCE APPROACH

Purpose

The Language Experience Approach (LEA) helps develop reading and writing through the use of students' own language, thoughts, and ideas. Students are able to read the stories with minimal cuing because they already know the meaning. The LEA does not require a specific level of proficiency in any language. Students working in a second language are able to develop at their own pace, using language they know and use in their own lives. It also opens a window to their cultures and ideas. It provides the teacher with a baseline for assessing the individual needs of the second-language learner. In a bilingual classroom it allows for choice of language.[4]

Procedure

This activity can be done with the whole class, a group, or individual students. Students will dictate a story to you. Follow these steps to execute the Language Experience Approach:

1. Conversation may suggest experience stories. The students may retell a news item, give a description of a job, game, toy, or an event happening in their life, or a sports story. A picture book with words covered is another resource.
2. The entire story is written (on the board, chart paper, overhead film, or computer) as the students speak. Alternatively, sticky note paper can be used to write the story and students can arrange sentences afterward. When working with the whole class or group, let students volunteer sentences. The name of the students can be placed next to their sentences.
3. Although the original approach recommends writing exactly what the students say, you can intervene on particular occasions to seize the opportunity to teach language. For example, Pedro dictated: "If I had magic, I will not clean the floor." The teacher, realizing that he was going to dictate other sentences explaining what else he would do, decided to teach him the use of the conditional. Before writing it down, she repeated the sentence correctly "If you had magic, you would not clean the floor?" and asked Pedro if he agreed. Because he nodded affirmatively, she wrote it correctly. For the following two sentences Pedro still used *will*. The teacher repeated the process. By the fourth sentence, Pedro, on his own, used *would*. Second-language learners need feedback if they are to learn the language.
4. Read the entire story to the students, point to individual words. Remember that precision in pointing is very important.
5. Reread a sentence, pointing to the words; then have the students read that sentence, pointing to the words.

---

[4]See Dixon and Nessel (1983), Peregoy and Boyle (1996), and Rigg (1989) for more information on this approach.

Follow-Up Activities

1. Pick out the meaningful words in the story. These words may be underlined. Write a word card for each of the words selected. Teach these
   words as sight words.
2. The students match their word cards with duplicates in the story, reading each word.
3. Either you or the students mix the cards, and the students read word
   cards independently. If they have trouble, they may match the word
   cards again with the story until they know several of them. Be satisfied
   with a reasonable number of words learned, depending on the students' abilities and learning paces.
4. Other word games can be played with these or other words or sentences from the story. These words may become a part of the students'
   vocabulary card-pack to be reviewed at your discretion.
5. The students may take their story and the word cards home.
6. You make a set of word cards.

The Approach in Practice:
Teaching Reading in the Special Education Resource Room[5]

The LEA proved to be a helpful approach for Laurie's first-grade student
Teddy. Although Teddy was born in the United States, his family speaks Greek
at home, and Teddy attends a Greek-language school in addition to attending a
monolingual English public school. Teddy had been referred for special education evaluation by his classroom teacher because of problems he experienced
maintaining on-task behavior. This lack of attention was very evident during
reading activities. He had difficulty with reading fluency and decoding, and
lacked knowledge of strategies to use when encountering such problems.
Laurie felt that the LEA might help Teddy increase his fluency and build up his
sight-word vocabulary.

Laurie began her sessions with Teddy by showing him several picture books.
She told him that he could pick whichever book he liked and that he was to write
a story about it. So that Teddy would not be distracted or intimidated by the
words on the page, Laurie covered the text of the story. Although the use of a
book is not necessarily part of the LEA , Laurie felt that it would help Teddy
maintain focus and develop a story sense. She also felt that using picture books
while covering the text of the story helped second-language learners focus on
making their own meaning for the story. Often, students new to United States
culture do not understand the content of the story.

---

[5]This project was carried out by Laurie Whitten.

After a few minutes discussing several books, Teddy chose *Milton the Early Riser*, by Kraus and began dictating his own story to Laurie, who wrote on yellow sticky papers. By writing the story on the sticky papers, Teddy was able to change the order of his story if he so chose. Both Laurie and Teddy read and re-read portions of the story as it developed. Laurie was careful to make sure that the words were pointed to as they were read. This first story and session with Teddy gave Laurie a good deal of information on words and sounds with which Teddy was having difficulty. She was able to note the sounds she should work on with Teddy and the words (such as *want, went,* and *with*), which he often confused. Because the focus of reading lessons in his classroom was a phonics-based approach, Laurie decided that she would work on context-based approaches to help Teddy with word identification.

In the following sessions, Laurie began transferring the sentences from the yellow sticky papers to sentence strips. Teddy participated by dictating the sentences to Laurie from the sticky papers. He was very motivated as he saw his story being displayed. He also made changes to his story, adding details and personal pronouns. For example, when adding the sentence "but the bear friends didn't answer him," to the story, Teddy changed it to "but *his* bear friends didn't answer him." If Teddy had difficulty with the words in the sentences, Laurie worked on using context clue strategies for him to read the words. Many times by reading the remainder of a sentence, Teddy was able to go back and read an unfamiliar word. Laurie found that an added benefit to Teddy's learning to read difficult words from context clues was that he was more inclined to read the sentence again, which increased his fluency skills. The rereading of the sentence was not what he usually did when he tried to decode a word. He usually just said the word and went on, but did not really comprehend what he had read.

Laurie did work on decoding skills with Teddy when he was very close to reading the word correctly. She sometimes cued him with the beginning sound. On words he confused frequently, she pointed out the differences in the beginning or ending sounds of the words. For example, he consistently confused the word *announcement* for *compliment*, probably because he had learned the word *compliment* and would say that word whenever he saw the "ment" ending. Laurie reminded him to look at the beginning sounds of the word, so that he would see that the word *announcement* could not be *compliment,* because it did not begin with a /k/ sound. After looking at the first two syllables, he was able to remember the word *announcement.*

She also used decoding strategies in helping Teddy distinguish between *want, went,* and *with.* He often needed to be cued to look at the letters and say the sounds. During one session, Laurie had Teddy go through the story he had written and color code the three words. After looking at all the words he had marked on the paper, he expressed how much work he had done! They then talked about the similarities and differences in the words, and Teddy began focusing on the middle sounds in each word. To reinforce the lesson, Laurie dictated sentences from the story, but omitted the three problem words. Teddy was to hold up the word card containing the correct word needed to complete the sentence. He was able to correctly use the word *with,* and improved his accuracy using the words *went* and *want.*

When they had completed transforming the story from the yellow sticky papers to sentences strips, Laurie used the text for cloze[6] and sequencing exercises. Teddy was able to fill in the missing words without having to refer to the story. She also made a smaller, typed version of the story in which Teddy drew illustrations.

When they had completed their book, Teddy read the original *Milton the Early Riser* book. He was able to read the first 12 pages with no problems, reading quite fluently, and easily recognizing many of the words. Teddy was also very interested in comparing his version of the story to the original.

In evaluating the success of the LEA with Teddy, Laurie found that there was a decrease in his guessing at words and that he was using decoding skills more. He also demonstrated an increase in the use of context clues to help him in his decoding. She observed better fluency in Teddy's reading, both of his own story and the original version of the story. Another positive outcome of the approach for Teddy was that he was able to stay on task for an extended period of time, 40 to 45 minutes.

Laurie believed that Teddy's reading abilities were better than what had previously been thought. What Teddy needed was a text and an environment that would motivate him to read. When provided with a text reflecting his ideas and language patterns, along with the encouragement to use other strategies beyond initial consonant sounds, both Teddy's fluency and interest increased.

STUDENT-DIRECTED SHARING TIME AND GROUP DISCUSSION

Purpose

Student-Directed Sharing Time and Group Discussions give students the practice of talking about something to an audience. Reading and writing activities can be done either before or after the oral activities to help students research information or reflect on what was discussed. It can be an opportune time for bilingual students to discuss issues relating to culture and language, for example, the struggles of living and studying in two cultures. This approach is easiest when students can use their stronger language. When they must speak in the second language, teachers have used helpful strategies such as deciding on top-

---

[6]This is a technique in which words (usually every fifth or seventh or so forth) in a sentence are omitted. Students are required to provide appropriate words to complete the sentence.

ics ahead of time, letting the students have notes to help the oral expression, and starting with a Semantic Map about the topic to provide vocabulary.[7]

Procedure

To execute the Sharing Time approach:
1. Choose an area of the room where the participants can sit in a circle. Explain to the students that every day they will gather around a leader and talk about something. It can be something that happened to them on the way to school, over the weekend, or a television program they saw, a newspaper or magazine article they read, and so forth.
2. Choose the leader of the day and have that student sit in a special chair. Start with those students who are more sure of themselves. The first day, you may want to model the role of the leader by taking the leader's chair and telling something that happened to you personally.
3. Give the rules (which should be reviewed occasionally):
   a. one person shares at a time
   b. leader chooses the person who speaks
   c. students have to raise their hand if they want to talk
   d. if students misbehave, they will get a warning (given by the leader, who also decides what "misbehaving" is)
   e. if given a second warning, students go to their seats.

To execute Group Discussions:
1. Divide the class into groups of 6 to 10 students, or work with the whole class.
2. Let the group decide on a list of topics that they would like to discuss for the term, or the month.
3. Before beginning the actual discussion, they may want to outline the topic. This outline, as well as reading and research, can be assigned as homework in preparation for the oral discussion.
4. Let students start the discussion. Give them a fixed amount of time to carry out the discussion. Assign a leader to help the flow of the discussion. If it is conducted in the nonnative language, students should feel free to ask a question, insert a word, or ask for a translation in their native language.

Follow-Up Activities:

1. Have students write an essay or summary of the topic discussed.
2. Have students read more on the topic discussed.

---

[7]See Savignon (1983) and Michaels and Foster (1985) for further information about this approach.

3. Tape record and transcribe sections of the discussion. Have students analyze their language. Follow up with lessons on specific language skills.

It is better to implement the discussions in cycles. For example, the group chooses four topics for the month. Each week they deal with a different topic. They discuss for 15 minutes every day for 3 days, the fourth day they write a summary, and the fifth day they bring their summaries for a final discussion. Leaders can be preassigned.

The Approach in Practice:
From Silent Spectators to Active Learners[8]

For Alice's 12 sixth-grade Haitian students, the Student-Directed Group Discussion approach provided a nonthreatening environment in which they could overcome their discomfort of speaking in public, and develop or increase pride and interest in their native culture. Alice implemented the Student-Directed Group Discussion Approach with the students, ages 11 through 14, twice a week during their Haitian Culture class. Because there were not many materials available in the school for that particular subject matter, Alice assigned the students a topic on which they researched using newspapers from Haiti, listening to radio programs, and interviewing family members. The topics to be covered included religion, family, life in Haiti, education, and politics. On the first day the students carried out a discussion session on the topic, then on the second day, Alice expanded on the topic using notes she had taken during the first day's discussion.

During the first session, the two speakers, Bervelyne and Nancy, spoke about religion and voodoo. Both stood in front of the class to make their presentations, Nancy speaking for about five minutes and Bervelyne nervously reading from a paper. Because there were no questions asked by the students after their presentation, Alice felt the need to add more information and ultimately took over the session. It was not until later that she realized that she had participated more than she should have, and had not encouraged the students to participate more. For the next session, she had the students sit in a circle. Although Alice made sure she did not take over the discussion, she still felt the need to monitor behavior and order in the group. Other students did participate in the discussion sharing their own thoughts and experiences on voodoo spirits. Esther shared her experience of living next to a person apparently possessed by voodoo spirits, and how she used to look through the keyholes in the door to see because children in her family were not permitted to look at such things.

Esther was the presenter at the next session. She spoke about the structure of the family as it is now in Haiti and how it was in the past. She explained that, in

---

[8]This project was carried out by Alice Kanel.

the past, the notion of family was different from what is thought of family nowadays. In the past, family could consist of father, mother, children, grandparents, aunts, uncles, and even longtime friends. She explained that at present, when one talks about family, it is usually mother, father, children and grandparents.

Esther also talked about the lakou system (i.e., several small houses are together on one piece of property and everyone lives like a family). She also talked about the previous monetary system, about which she had learned from her grandmother. The other students seemed very interested in her presentation and asked many questions. Occasionally, during the discussion, students directed their question to Alice, who suggested that the questions be asked of another student.

Even though this particular session was a bit more integrative and participatory, Alice believed that they were becoming too much of a question and answer period with the presenter being seen as an expert on the topic, or being challenged for what she had said. Alice, therefore, reviewed the idea of Student-Directed Group Discussion, went over the protocol of the discussion (i.e., raise your hand to make a comment, wait your turn to speak, and so forth). She also decided to have a monitor for each session who assisted the leader in making sure the discussion was orderly and everyone had an opportunity to share.

As the Student-Directed Group Discussion sessions continued, the students became more comfortable with the format. They observed the rules of the group, turning to the monitor when they wished to speak. They joined in on the discussions, relating the topic to their personal experiences. Darline and Jean Ralph spoke about life in Haiti. Because neither was well prepared for the topic, other students took over the lead. Hans explained that there were two classes of people in Haiti, those with lots of money and those with no money. He went on to explain that because the poorer people did not have money, they exchanged goods and services instead. He told the group that people in the village helped each other during bad times. This statement reminded Jean Ralph of a good friend he had in Haiti with whom he shared many things. Other students then spoke about their experiences living in Haiti. Sometime during the discussion, Esther began to talk again about voodoo. The monitor interrupted and reminded the group that religion was not the topic currently being discussed.

It was during the topic of education that Alice saw growth in how the students discussed issues, and how comfortable they were in expressing their opinions. The students were speaking about schools in Haiti, and in particular, teachers in Haiti and their use of corporal punishment, which was allowed by law. Darline spoke about her first-grade teacher:

> I will never forget that teacher I had in (*preparatoire* I) first grade. She was so mean, she used to hit us with a ruler on our knuckles.[9]

---

[9]All discussions were carried out in Haitian Creole.

Esther had a different opinion of the schools in Haiti. She stated:

> In Haiti the teachers are very strict but the students respect them. But here in
> _____, the students say anything they want to the teachers. They are so disre-
> spectful.

The discussion of schools and the Haitian education system continued. Alice learned a lot about the students just from listening to them talk about their
experiences in school in Haiti. She learned that many of her students were from
rural schools, where the school experience is quite different from students attending school in the city. She was surprised that the students even admitted
having attended a rural school, because they usually were embarrassed to say
that they were from the country. Alice believed, however, that the sense of community and trust was strong enough in the group, that the students did not hesi-
tate to talk about their lives.

The political situation in Haiti at the time was also an important topic of discussion for the students. They were involved in discussing the election that was
to take place soon in Haiti. Nancy began the discussion by talking about what
she had heard on the radio about the election:

> I heard that twelve of the candidates were eliminated. There will be an election on
> November 29th where people will be going to the polls for the first time in 30
> years to elect a new president. A few months ago the Junta said that they will al-
> low Haitians who live outside the country to vote, but now I think they have
> changed their mind. My parents said they don't think the election will take place
> because of all the turmoil ...

Others joined in. Sandy stated:

> Well, I hope there is an election so they can stop killing people.

Hans then remarked:

> If we had a revolution this would not have happened, everything would have been
> fine by now. It is two years, two years since Duvalier left and nothing has
> changed.

Jean Ralph replied:

> Well, it is the same for the C.N.G. (National Council of Goverment). The Haitian
> people had no objection at the beginning but when they realized the C.N.G. was a
> continuation of the Duvalier's regime they turned against it.

In reviewing the overall effects of the Student-Directed Group Discussion
approach on the goal of increasing students' ability to speak in public, Alice
saw a marked improvement. The students no longer waited for her to initiate a
discussion. They expressed their opinions about a topic, and challenged the
comments of others. One of the students even asked Alice if she would take

them to the library so that they could better research their topics. Alice believed that the Student-Directed Group Discussion encouraged the students to become more interested in their native culture and the politics of Haiti. This project involved the families as well. Much of the information was secured through interviews with family members.

Once the students in Alice's other classes heard about the discussions that took place, they also asked Alice if she would conduct that type of lesson in their classes. The students began to see Alice as a person they could trust and approached her frequently to discuss many other issues.

COOPERATIVE LEARNING: JIGSAW

Purpose

The Jigsaw approach is a way for students to work cooperatively and help each other to learn new material. Students take an active role in their learning as they teach other students what they have learned. In a bilingual setting, students have the opportunity to learn appropriate vocabulary in both languages. For second-language learners, this approach helps lessen the burden of trying to understand a large amount of expository text in a short amount of time.[10]

Procedure

To execute the Jigsaw approach:

1. Divide material into sections. (For example, divide a reading into four sections).
2. Have students form groups with as many students per group as sections of material. (For example, for a reading selection divided into four sections, there will be four students in each group.)
3. Ask each group to send one member to an "expert" group where one section of the material will be read, discussed, and learned. Each group should know where in the whole material their section fits. (In the example, there will be four expert groups with one student from each of the original groups.)
4. Once the students have learned the material, have them return to their original group and report to those students what they have learned.
5. After all students have taught the other members of their original group the material in which they are expert, have students do an activity individually in which they show how much of the material they have learned. (For example, write individually a summary of the *whole* reading.)

---

[10]See Kagan (1992) and Pardon (1992) for further information about this approach and other cooperative learning approaches.

The Approach in Practice:
All the Pieces of the Puzzle Fit Together![11]

The Jigsaw approach proved to be an effective way for Peggy's third- and fourth-grade Spanish bilingual students to learn about the events leading to the American Revolution. The class is comprised of 16 third-grade and 11 fourth-grade students in a transitional bilingual classroom with myriad levels of language proficiency and literacy development. Spanish is the first language of all the students. The English language proficiency, however, varies from very low oral language proficiency in English to near mastery. Many students are at or near grade level in reading (both in English and Spanish), whereas others are still developing their literacy skills in Spanish. Others are beginning to adapt and transfer skills learned in Spanish to English reading. Although many of the students are recent immigrants to the United States and began their literacy development in their native country, quite a few students were born in the United States and have learned how to read and write in bilingual programs in this country.

Peggy began working on the approach by discussing with the whole class the relationship between the colonists and the king of England. She wanted the students to understand that although the colonists expressed loyalty to the king of England, they also felt that their way of living was very different from the way people lived in England, and that they should have more of a voice in how America would be governed. She asked individual students who were born in the United States to identify their national heritage. Justina claimed she was Dominican, and Marcos said he was American. Julie then agreed that she, too, was American, but also Dominican. This led to a discussion of how different people feel about their allegiances to countries, and whether people could be loyal to two countries at the same time. The students also discussed the differences in lifestyle between their native country and the United States, and how it was often difficult for people living in one country to understand the way life was in another.

The students were placed heterogeneously into five groups, five students to a group. Because there were two more students than places needed, Peggy paired the two least-strong readers with another person and asked them to work together.

She then explained the Jigsaw method to the students. They were told that the Jigsaw method was a way for the students to work together and teach each other new material. She discussed the logistics of the Jigsaw. She wrote five major themes on the board (in both English and Spanish): Taxes, Laws, Boston, Continental Congress, and Declaration of Independence. One student from each group chose a theme. They were told that they would become the "expert"

---

[11]This project was carried out by Margaret (Peggy) Harrington.

on the theme they had chosen; that they would read about it and discuss it with students from the other groups, and then report what they had learned to their original group. It took a few minutes for the students to completely understand the concept. Even after they had been working in the "expert" groups for a few minutes, some students were still confused. Eventually, all understood and the pieces of the jigsaw puzzle were fitting together.

For resources, the students were provided with materials in both English and Spanish, including social studies textbooks, copies of short essays about the particular themes, and other books. Unfortunately, there were many more materials in English than in Spanish. The social studies book in Spanish, however, did have a lot of good information for the students. They were given all the materials and could choose to read in Spanish or English, or both. The students then began reading their information. They were allowed to read either alone, or with one or two other students. Most chose to partner with someone else. Clara chose to read the material in English, but when she wanted to comment on what was read, she usually did so in Spanish. Her explanations in Spanish were a lot more detailed and descriptive.

When all the students had finished reading the materials, they were called back to their expert groups to discuss what they had read. Peggy walked from group to group during the discussions to assure that the students understood the material and to clarify any misunderstandings.

The students' individual styles of learning were evident during the discussion. Some students had written down important facts in order to remember them, other students had underlined important paragraphs in the materials they had read and referred to them during the discussion.

The discussions were lively with lots of switching back and forth from English to Spanish. Juana had read her material in English, but spoke both English and Spanish in the group, because she knew that some of the members of her group would understand better if she explained what she had learned in Spanish. Francisco, a dominant Spanish-speaker, intensely read the material in Spanish, but also read the other information in English and referred to it during the discussion. The students worked in their expert groups until they determined that they knew their material well and were ready to teach what they had learned to their original groups. For homework that night the students were told to write a summary of their theme, which they then read, or used as a reference, when teaching to their group the next day.

The students were reminded that although they had learned about only one aspect of the topic being studied, they were responsible for knowing all the material, and that they as a group needed to ensure that all members explained their themes well enough for all to understand. The student experts then returned to their original groups to report on what they had learned. Most students had prepared their summaries for homework the night before and chose to read what they had written.

The students read their summaries. While Mercedes was reading hers, students in the group noted some errors in what she was saying about the taxes imposed on the colonists, which led to the students referring to the material to verify the information. After Francisco had read his summary, he questioned the students in his group about what he had just read to make sure they understood what he was explaining. When he felt that they had not understood well enough, he elaborated on the point.

For some students, it was very difficult to either write a summary or read it out loud. Leslie, who has difficulty reading, did not come prepared with a written summary. The students called Peggy over to complain about her not being prepared. Peggy suggested to the group that they ask Leslie what she could tell them about her theme (taxes). Once Leslie began talking , she was able to explain a little of what she had read. Because Leslie had been partnered with another student, the students learned additional information about the theme from Gloria. Sandra, who is extemely shy, did not want to speak at all when it was her turn to read her summary. It took some convincing from the other students before she felt comfortable enough to read her summary. Once she felt comfortable with her group though, she did an excellent job of explaining her theme, and the other members of her group let her know that. The students in Juan's group complained about the lack of information in his summary. Juan knew he had let his group down and promised to work on a better summary that night for homework.

Often during the presentation of someone's theme, other students in the group commented to the presenter, adding information or clarifying a point. While Ana was explaining about the Stamp Act, Mercedes added her explanation of taxes to help the group understand better. At other times, students intervened to help if the student could not think of a good way to explain something. The students in the groups also began to see connections between what they had read about and what the other students in the group had explained. Clara, who had studied about the occurrences in Boston, began to see the relationship between what happened there to the laws imposed on the colonists. She said she now understood why the people in Boston were so angry.

Although there was no assigned leader to any group, it seemed that one person in most of the groups took over that role. Patricia easily took on the role as facilitator, making sure all had the opportunity to read their summaries and respond to comments. Clara saw to it that everyone was listening to the speaker in her group. During the summary readings in his group, Francisco often stopped and asked someone a question to see if they had been listening.

Because the groups did not all finish their summary readings at the same time, it was suggested to those that had finished that they either ask each other questions about their themes, or try to work on some of the questions found in the social studies textbooks as a way of reviewing the information learned.

In order to give the students an opportunity to tie all five themes together, Peggy assigned for homework a quick reading of the chapter. The students were told just to read through the chapter once, not worrying so much about detail, as much as seeing how one event affected the other.

To assess the students' individual understanding of the material, Peggy created a scenario in which the students were to imagine that they were living in Boston in the 1770s and had just received a letter from their grandfather or grandmother who was living in England. The grandparent had sent the letter in order to find out why the colonists would ever disobey their king. Each student was to respond to his or her grandparent's letter, explaining why the colonists were rebelling against the king. The students were given the option of being for or against the colonists' cause, but in their letter they had to explain in detail the five points covered during their Jigsaw method. They were allowed to use their books and other materials as points of reference when writing their letter.

Patricia dated her letter about a week after the Declaration of Independence had been signed (the English translation follows):

7/10/76

Querida Abuela,
Aqui en Boston esta matando personas y ahi muchos problemas. Yo se que tu quiere a tu rey pero haora el esta muy malo y tenemos que pagar Impuestos. En inglatera no esta pasando nada pero haqui esta pasando muchas cosa mala el. rey esta muy malo. Paraca casi no hay comida y todos los soldados esta cojiendo la comida y las camas aqui mataro cinco hombres y despues dos. Por que tiraron el te en el agua hay muchos problemas. Le estan mandando cartas al rey pero el no la contesta. Aya en inglatera viviendo bien poro paraca no. El 4 de julio mandaron una carta de Independencia pero el rey no le iso caso como las otras cartas.
En el comienso estaba fasil pero haora esta duro no hay comida ni hay camas y esta una gera como bamos a vivir aqui. El rey sepuso bien brabo cuado le tiraron 351 caja de te. Haqui todas la jentes se esta muriendo. aqui no esta fasil.
Sinceramente,

Dear Grandmother,
Here in Boston they are killing people and that are a lot of problems. I know that you love your king, but now he is bad and we have to pay taxes. In England nothing is happening, but here a lot of bad things are happening. The king is very mean. Here there is no food and all the soldiers are taking our food and beds. Here they killed five men and later two. Because they threw tea in the water they are many problems. They are sending letters to the king, but he doesn't answer them. There in England they are living well, but here no. On July 4 they sent a letter to the king, but he paid no attention, just like the other letters.
In the beginning it was easy, but now it is hard. There is no food, no beds, and we are going to be living in a war here. The king was very angry when they threw the 351 boxes of tea overboard. Everyone here is dying. It is not easy.
Sincerely,

By reading the letters, Peggy was able to tell which students understood most of the material, those that were confused on some issues, and the others who did not seem to understand the basic ideas of the themes. Although the majority of students did grasp the main ideas of the unit, some students did not. Sandra, for example, seemed confused about where the colonists lived. She kept referring to how difficult life and the laws were in England. Ana did not seem to understand that she was writing a realistic letter about historical events. She wrote a story as if it were a fairy tale.

Peggy asked the students how they liked learning social studies using the Jigsaw method. Clara said that she liked it because she got to work with other students, and did not have to read the material alone. Francisco liked the idea of learning from his fellow students. Justina felt that it helped her learn better, because she could learn a lot of material without having to read so much.

CROSS-AGE PROJECT

Purpose

The purpose of this approach is to help older students with learning difficulties by making them teachers of younger students in precisely the area they are experiencing difficulty, such as reading in the native language or English, math, science, and so on. The children are actively involved in their own learning as they practice reading, asking questions, and internalizing the strategies they use to work with the younger children. This approach is helpful for bilingual learners because it allows them to focus on the development of literacy in one of their languages based on their needs. Older students can work on basic skills without feeling that they are being treated as slow or beginners. In learning how to be teachers, they familiarize themselves with learning strategies.

This approach provides a natural setting for integrating students of different language backgrounds. Teachers of older bilingual students can arrange a Cross-Age Project with a class of younger monolingual students. Also, older bilingual students can serve as role models when working with younger bilingual students. Both these contexts make bilinguals proud of their language skills. This approach also gives the younger students individual attention.[12]

Procedure

Follow these steps to conduct a Cross-Age Project:
1. Choose two classes, one with students older than the other.
2. Explain to both classes what the project is all about. Introduce the classes to each other through an activity.
3. Start working with the older students by doing the following:
   a. Model the chosen method or approach.
   b. Train, explain, and discuss the method with students.
   c. Let them rehearse with each other and do any preparation needed.

---

[12]See Freeman and Freeman (1998), Juel (1991), Labbo and Teale (1990) and Urzua (1995) for further information about this project.

4. At all times, the older learners should keep a journal in which they reflect, first about the training, later about the actual experience as teachers.
5. Read and respond to the journals. Steps 1–5 should take a minimum of two to three weeks to ensure that the older students are ready.
6. When the "teachers" (older students) are ready, start implementation.
7. Pair the older with the younger students. If the classes are uneven, some groups may be larger than two. Divide the two classes into two groups. Each group stays with one of the two teachers involved.
8. Allow for follow-up activities as they naturally develop at the initiative of students.
9. Plan other activities such as parties or field trips that they can do together.
10. Meet with the "teachers" periodically to discuss how the implementation is going, as well as the content and process of learning. Focus especially on the older learners' needs.

The Approach in Practice:
Bilingual Fifth Graders Become Reading Teachers[13]

A Cross-Age Project was initiated between Eileen's fifth-grade transitional Spanish bilingual classroom and a monolingual English first grade. The main purpose for the project was to create an atmosphere for authentic reading and writing activities in the second language (English) for the fifth graders, while giving individual attention and opportunities for hearing stories read aloud to the younger children.

The fifth-grade students were in the last year of their bilingual program, many of them having been in the program for less than three years. All their subjects were taught in English in order to prepare them for mainstream classes the following year. Although the students' listening and speaking skills were advanced, their average reading grade level was 3.7. The first graders were students who were in a "readiness" class that could be considered a transitional class between kindergarten and first grade. It was felt that both classes would benefit from the Cross-Age Project.

The teachers began the project by introducing the idea to the fifth graders who responded enthusiastically to it. They had already worked on making a big book with that particular first-grade class, so a relationship between the students had already been formed. They were told how important their preparation was for the success of the project. The teachers began by reading children's stories to the fifth graders. The children listened to the teacher reading a story aloud and then wrote in journals about various aspects of the project (i.e., the

---

[13]This project was carried out by Mary Eileen Skovholt.

stories read to them, being read to aloud, etc.). The teachers then responded to the journals.

The classroom teachers chose folk tales as the stories they would read to the fifth graders to prepare them to become the teachers. They felt that the content of the stories was appropriate for both age groups, that it would hold the interest of the older students, and that the illustrations would help elaborate the meanings of the tales. During these read-alouds the teachers concentrated on modeling techniques that the older students would use when they were the "teachers." They asked questions to monitor comprehension, help make predictions, elicit prior knowledge, and make the important connections to the children's own experiences.

Although hesitant at first to read aloud to the fifth graders, thinking that they would not enjoy such an activity, the teachers soon discovered that fifth graders reacted positively to listening to stories read aloud. Excerpts from the students' journals corroborate this finding:

> Today we listened to a story it was called *Who's in Rabbit's House.* I liked the story because of the frog and how he laughed. I also like when the caterpillar came out of the house. I really liked that story and I hope I hear or read a good story like: *Who's in Rabbit's House.* (Mitchell)
>
> I liked the story because it was good and it was sad because they didn't have food at the end and I would like to read it again to the little kids. Someday I would like to read this book again. Can you read it again? (Gisela)

The students wrote in their journals after each story read aloud. This activity allowed the students to not only reflect on the story, but also to relate the story to their personal experiences and feelings. They were able to critique the stories that were read, suggest alternative endings, and so on. The teachers found that the journal entries were rich with discussions about the favorite parts of the story, whether the story could be true, and how they could relate what happened in the story to their own lives, an important connection for comprehension and the joy of reading. Mitchell wrote in his journal about his liking scary stories:

> Today I checked out a book. *Ghost's Hour, Spook's Hour.* I liked beautiful stories but one of my favorites is scary stories. I like scary because I like to be scared. I don't know what's inside me that makes me feel that way.

By writing in the journal, Mitchell was able to reflect on his feelings about the story, and share his reaction to the stories read. Another student, Ana, connected the story of *The Ugly Duckling* to experiences she had when living in Puerto Rico:

> I liked the part when the duck didn't know that he was a swan and he saw his reflection on the water. And I thought he was going back with his mom. In Puerto Rico I had a man chicken and a hen and I have ducklings but they were all beautiful ...

Efrain became the expert when he was able to explain to the class, because of his experiences in Puerto Rico, why the mother hen sits on her eggs.

The teachers continued the read-aloud modeling twice a week for five weeks. They felt that each student needed the time to prepare for his or her role as teacher. The help of the school librarian was solicited during the fourth week of the project to show the fifth graders appropriate books for first graders. She showed them examples of appropriate children's literature and explained how to look for suitable books (e.g., predictable books, rhyming books, and picture books). She also modeled for the students, showing them different techniques they could use when reading aloud, and explained why the strategies were important. The students displayed their understanding of the modeling done by the librarian through their journal entries:

> The book I picked to practice is *Three by the Sea*. ... the book they read in the library was a good story. We have to read easy books to the children so that they could understand and phrases repeat and sound and pictures so that they enjoy the book just like we enjoy a book. (Wanda)
> Today I was in the library. I learned how to express my feelings when I read a book and how to show them the picture and tell what's happening in the picture. It was nice to know about books. (Marta)

During the fifth week of the project the fifth-grade students began to read to each other for practice. They had selected the first book they were planning to read with the younger children. They asked their partners questions using the strategies they had learned from the teachers when they were reading aloud. The partners being read to also had the opportunity to role play and ask questions of the reader. This experience provided the students with authentic purposes for reading and a deeper awareness of the purpose of reading. Many students expressed that they learned more and enjoyed reading more when they were able to share the experience with a peer.

When the students were ready to read to their first-grade partners, each class was divided into two groups. One half of each class read in their own classroom while the other half visited the other classroom. It was planned that halfway through the project the groups would switch so that everyone had the chance to visit both classrooms. The teachers decided to let the children "naturally" pick their partner. Because each class had the same number of students, there was no problem with pairing up. The fifth graders seemed to just walk over to their partner. The students spent 30 minutes reading. After returning to their classes, the fifth graders spent another 20 minutes writing about the experience in their journals. The journal entries reflected many positive feelings that the fifth graders had about the read-aloud. They expressed a sense of responsibility to their charges:

> I like reading to Luis because he listens to me and he gave me some sentences. He drew me a dinosaur and I taught him how to write the word "strong."

The book I read the is *Little Monster's Neighborhood*. It was about little monsters and Luis laugh and he was very happy. I drew him a bird and he said, "You are my best teacher." So I was happy to read to him. I hope he won't be absent. (Raul)

They also understood the importance of selecting appropriate reading material, that is, books that their partners preferred:

I read to BJ *All My Toys are on the Floor*. I like the story and BJ did not kind of like it so next time I will read him a better thing than that. (Efraín)

As the project continued, the confidence of the students increased and they began to initiate other activities with their partners. They had the first graders pick out the book they wanted read, or had the first grader act out part of the story. Observations of the first graders showed that they were beginning to mimic the modeling techniques done by their fifth-grade partners.

Writing became part of the activities. The first graders drew a picture related to the story after having heard it read aloud. Some first graders even wrote about the story, or dictated a sentence to their partner.

The project proved to be enjoyable and important for the first graders as well. During a class assignment, the students had to respond to the prompt: "I have a good day when…" Most of the students responded by saying, "My partner reads to me." When interviewed at the end of the project as to whether they liked being read to, Christina replied, "I think it's nice for kids who know how to read to show little kids how to read."

The culminating activity was a field trip for both classes to Boston Public Gardens, which has a special tour designed around the book, *Make Way for Ducklings* by McCloskey. Each student received a copy of the book that was signed by their partner as a remembrance of the special bond between them.

Through an interview done at the end of the project, the fifth-grade students expressed that they felt that they themselves had become better readers by reading to the first graders. They explained the strategies they used to help them become better readers. For example, Gisela stated: "Well I used to read very fast and I learned how to stop when there is a period, etc." And Juan said: "How the little kids learned helped me myself to read better." Edison clearly shows satisfaction with his progress: "To read with expression, to get into books, learn words, made me happier."

Eileen noticed an increase in the quantity of reading done by the students once they became involved in the Cross-Age project. They became more interested in books for their own pleasure, and were more careful in selecting books. She attributes this to the increase in self-confidence and motivation the students gained by working with the first graders. Efrain comments: "I learned to read better. I took two books, one for me and one for the little kid."

The students also demonstrated a better understanding of the writing process and its relation to reading. Juana commented in her journal: "Writing

helped me think about things because you write down everything that happened with the little children." Melissa stated: "Now I understand more about
reading. After when I write it, I read it again."

The Cross-Age Project is a win–win situation. The older students learn the
importance of reading, and can increase their confidence and skills in both
reading and writing. The younger students are given some "special" attention
and also have excellent role models in the older students.

CRITICAL AUTOBIOGRAPHIES

Purpose

The purpose of this approach is to have students look critically and objectively
at events in their lives that affect them as bilingual individuals. Through this
analysis they will understand that what happens to them as bilingual individuals struggling with social and cultural adjustment is largely governed by circumstances outside themselves. The key to bringing about change is the
discussion and other activities that help analyze the students' situations. The
activities involving the exploration of issues require that students read and discuss for an authentic purpose and that they write extended text of great interest
to them. Exploration of the topics affects the students' perception of themselves in their bilingual–bicultural context, whereas the numerous activities
they carry out develop their literacy ability in meaningful ways.[14]

Procedure

Following is the procedure for the Critical Autobiographies approach:

1. Introduction of the Project
   To younger students (Grades K–2), explain that they are going to write
   about their lives in different countries or about the culture of their parents. It will be a chapter book about themselves, their families, and the
   countries where they have lived.
   To older students (Grades 3–12), introduce the concept of a biography
   and autobiography. Have them read biographies and autobiographies.
   Discuss them. Do other activities to familiarize them with this type of
   genre.
2. Exploration of Themes
   Explore external factors and issues of concern for the students through
   different activities. These activities can be an integral part of the curriculum of language arts, reading, and content areas. Depending on the
   age or grade level of the students, use activities such as:

---

[14]See Benesch (1993), Brisk (1998b), Brisk and Zandman (1995), and Wallerstein (1983) for
further information about this approach.

- Reading books about students' countries, stories about immigrant children, and other relevant topics that will stimulate thinking. You can read them aloud or let the students read them in groups or individually.
- Writing response journals.
- Developing questionnaires to interview families, each other, other students, or staff in the school.
- Bringing speakers (including family members) with immigrant experiences.
- Having open discussions about topics of concern.
- Doing surveys about topics of concern.
- Studying the sociopolitical history of ethnic groups.
- Doing attitudinal surveys among mainstream students and staff.
- Doing comparisons between characteristics of the country of origin and the country of residence.

These activities are directed to elicit discussion and thinking around linguistic, cultural, economic, political, and social factors or aim at exploring objectively, and in depth, issues raised by the students. This exploration can be done during prewriting activities as well as during writing and revising. Parents and other family members should be involved to clarify and contribute to the discussion and information sharing.

3. Writing the Autobiographies

   Younger students draw and dictate their stories. Type drafts and read them with the students for additions and revisions. Older students use a process approach to writing. They write drafts, revise, and edit their work. If there is access to computers, it is best to use computers from the earliest stages.

4. Publication of Books

   Students produce chapter books or several books that contain the work they have done.

The Approach in Practice:
Sixth-Graders Write Critical Autobriographies[15]

Carmen implemented the Critical Autobiography approach, embedding the activities within the language arts and social studies curriculum in a sixth-grade Spanish bilingual classroom. Because her students had been in the United States less than a year, she conducted the entire project in Spanish. All the activities were carried out with the class as a whole with constant discussion among the whole class. The written products that emerged were revised, laminated, and assembled in a portfolio.

---

[15]This project was carried out by Carmen C. Alvarez.

Carmen introduced the project by having students define the concept of *autobiography*. Collectively, the students brainstormed ideas of topics to include in their autobiographies. They agreed on nine and organized them sequentially. Topics were:

1. Reason why they are in the country
2. The trip to the United States
3. The first day of school in the United States
4. Their first friend and why
5. Learning English and speaking Spanish
6. The family here
7. The family in the native country
8. My old country
9. My life today, yesterday, and in the future

Each student kept a list to check as he or she was completing each chapter. The list also remained on a corner of the board for the duration of the project. For each topic, Carmen prepared an activity to stimulate discussion. After each activity, students wrote an essay for the corresponding chapter.

In order to stimulate thoughts about themselves, Carmen had the students read and analyze the poem, *Yo soy como el rio* (I Am Like the River), by Alexander Otero Cruz, 11 years old, from Puerto Rico (the English translation follows):

Yo soy como el río
que llega y se va,
con su hermoso ruido
y con su claridad.
Yo soy como el río:
algunas veces tranquilo
y otras ni aguantarme pueden,
pero traigo diversiones
y a los niños day afán.
Yo soy como el río,
no me parezco al mar
porque yo soy muy dulce,
y él está lleno de sal.

I am like the river
which comes and goes
with its beautiful noise
and with its clarity.
I am like the river:
sometimes tranquil
and at other times they can't even contain me,
but I bring entertainment
and to the children I give hard work.
I am like the river,

I am not like the sea,
because I am very sweet
and the sea is full of salt.

Students then chose an object and wrote their own poems comparing themselves with that object.

A professional Honduran woman was invited to come to speak to the students about her immigrant experience. In preparation for the visit, Carmen told
the students briefly about her. Students wrote down questions for her, mostly
based on the topics for their autobiography. On the day of the visit, students
posed such questions as: ¿De qué país viene? (Where do you come from?); ¿La
gente te mira cuando hablas español? (Do people look at you when you speak
Spanish?); ¿Cómo te sentías cuando te dijeron que venías a los Estados
Unidos? (How did you feel when they told you that you were coming to the
United States?) ¿Te recuerdas de tu primer amiga americana? (Do you remember your first American friend?) ¿Cómo te fue el primer día de escuela? (How
did your first day of school go?)

The students followed up the visit with a discussion comparing themselves
with the visitor. They found hope in the comparison, but also they felt free to
express pain. Christian pointed out that because they had arrived at a younger
age, they had more time to learn English and become just as successful as she is,
while another student wrote that "Lo mio se parese a lo de ella porque también
en la primera escuela hubo problemas ... también mi cultura ... también a mi
me faltan mis amigos porque ellos me hacían compañía más que los amigos de
aquí." (My case is similar to hers because in my first school there were problems ... also with my culture ... also I miss my friends because they kept me
company better than the ones here.) The visit and following discussion stimu-
lated ideas for several of the chapters.

To explore additional issues the teacher prepared a questionnaire, based on
the situational factors, to be used by the students in interviewing their families.
Students wrote the responses and brought these to class to share and discuss. To
the question on reasons for immigrating, families cited health, education, re-
uniting with family, and economic mobility. The issue of how life had changed
was explained by language, culture, independence, workload, and financial situation. Other topics explored through this questionnaire were memories of
their native country and the struggles they were experiencing in the United
States. Most students noticed the emotional reactions of their relatives to these
interview questions. Denis wrote, "Mi mamá se puso felis triste al recordarse
de my familia" (My mother felt happy and sad remembering her family).

For the next activity, the students chose a partner, by pulling a name from a
bag, to interview on issues of language use. These students used English in "la
piscina y los centros de diverciones," "el supermercado, el centro donde se
vende peliculas," "en la casa del padrastro" (at the swimming pool, community

centers, supermarket, video stores, school, stepfather's house) as well as other relatives' houses. They all agreed on school as a place where they practice and hear a lot of English.

Most students felt high motivation to learn English in order to "superarse, defenderse, para tener un buen trabajo, para estudiar, para viajar, para conocer amistades que hablan inglés, para aprender en la escuela" (to improve, defend oneself, have a good job, study, travel, meet people who speak English, learn in school). Some students thought it was difficult to learn and they didn't like it. One student did not want to learn because he was intending to return to his native country.

Students said they used Spanish when they were in their own Latin community, as well as other Latin communities, and the neighborhood stores and restaurants. Students began to express the realization of their bilingualism and language needs: "Hablar español es un orgullo para mí, pero aquí me toca hablar inglés," (I'm proud of being able to speak Spanish, but here I must speak English).

Students wrote essays in relation to each of the nine themes established at the start of the program. Previously described activities, teacher modeling, and class discussion elicited ideas to be included in the essays. As the students wrote, the teacher circulated clarifying, stimulating more writing, and assisting students. Carmen responded to the first drafts. Students made revisions and prepared final versions.

The essays revealed some general information about these students, such as their country of origin, age, hobbies, and favorite foods. They also served as a forum for analysis and discussion of issues affecting these students, such as the reluctance to leave their home country, the problems created by separating from family members: "yo quería quedarme con mi abuela" (I wanted to stay with my grandmother); and the initial excitement of being in a new place, followed by a feeling of loneliness: "cuando lege aqui etaba contento al principio, pero empeze a rializar que no conocia a nadie" (when I arrived I was initially happy, but then I realized I didn't know anybody).

One student wrote about the fears and frustrations of being in a new school with people speaking a strange language who considered him odd: "cuando llegué a la escuela sentí un poco de miedo" (when I came to school, I was a little afraid), "mis amigos hablaban inglés pero yo me sentía raro ... y todos me miraban ... " (my friends spoke English and I felt strange ... they all looked at me ...). Others felt that the schools were friendly and helpful: "Me gusta mucho este estado por sus personas y las escuelas ayudan mucho" (I like this state for its people and the schools help a lot).

Students wrote essays about their very complicated family situations. These students live with some family, not always the two parents, have family in the vicinity, in other states, and still a considerable number of relatives in their country of origin. They expressed longing: "Cuando duermo siempre pienso en ellos" (when I sleep I always think about them); and frustrations experienced by some relatives: "A algunos familiares no les gusta este país por el clima es muy frío" (Some relatives don't like this country because of the cold weather).

Instead of writing an essay about the country of origin, the students decided they wanted to make a picture. Carmen encouraged them to write a short caption explaining the drawing. Rather than a pragmatic description of their countries, the students drew happy and sad memories they had. Henry drew a happy and colorful scene, while Victor drew a lonely child at the beach. Some probing revealed that his mother had died and the father had left the grandmother in charge of the family.

Often during class discussions, issues came up that Carmen felt needed discussion and resolution. For example, Christian declared, "Todos los morenos son malos y venden drogas" (all Blacks are bad and sell drugs). Carmen asked them questions such as, "How many know African Americans that work? How many know Latin drug dealers?" After a discussion, one of the students declared: "pero cada tipo de gente tiene gente mala" (all types of people have bad people). Students complained one day that other students in the school looked at them funny when they were speaking Spanish. Through questioning, students discovered that they themselves looked strange at the Vietnamese students in the school when they were speaking Vietnamese. They concluded that it was not such an atypical behavior and they probably shouldn't worry about it too much.

There were plenty of opportunities for teaching American culture. When one student complained about having to wait for a bus in the cold weather, they all inquired about being bused to schools far from their homes. The teacher went on to explain about segregation, the civil rights movement, and Rosa Parks. The students were shocked by the revelations of this aspect of American history and culture.

When Carmen was approached by a Spanish high school teacher to start a pen pal project, the students were ready to talk about themselves, their countries, and issues of concern to them. They wrote freely and with enthusiasm in spite of the fact that they noticed that their pen pals had written all their letters on computers and it was obvious to them that they came from a more affluent environment.

This approach was beneficial to Carmen and her students for many reasons. It enriched Carmen's language arts and social studies curriculum. It helped her learn about her students. The students practiced discussion skills as well as writing and thinking skills.

5

Implementation and Assessment

Good literacy practices are not enough to develop literacy when students function in more than one language and culture. Teachers must take a bilingual approach to teaching and assessment to provide quality instruction and fair assessment. They must know their students as bilingual learners even if they themselves know only one language and are charged with teaching in one language.

Implementation of the approaches recommended in this book requires teachers to:

- Learn about each individual student.
- Take a bilingual–bicultural approach to literacy instruction.
- Connect assessment and instruction.

LEARNING ABOUT STUDENTS

Bilingual students' learning is influenced by personal, home, and situational factors. Knowledge of students is key to good literacy instruction. Teachers are better able to teach, motivate, and evaluate students when they know about them, their families, and their environments. They also need to know them specifically as readers and writers. Teachers, when possible, should use both languages to learn about their students because people tend to reveal different things when using one or the other language.

Students are individuals very different from each other. No assumptions should be made by their last name or physical characteristics. Linda, a bilingual ASL/English teacher, works with four severely handicapped children who also are deaf or hard of hearing. Although in a program for deaf children, they all have completely different language backgrounds. Haitian Creole is the home language for one child and English for another. English is spoken in the home of one of the Spanish-background children and Spanish is the home language of the other. Similarly, families show complete difference in ASL ability, from none, to some signs, to fluency by at least one member of the family.

Demographic information clusters ethnic groups as Hispanic, Asian, and so forth. Within those clusters, however, there are very different cultural groups. Bilingual learners should be known not as Hispanic but as Puerto Rican, Colombian, or Salvadoran. Among Asians, Korean, Japanese, and Chinese represent very different cultural groups. Students themselves do not appreciate this confusion. "Most of my friends think I'm Chinese, because I look like a Chinese person. Some think I'm Japanese. I like being Korean ... " expressed Rose with annoyance.

Bilingual students may receive different language input in the various contexts in which they function. The amount of language use and support they receive in these various contexts will influence development of each language. Teachers need to know which language bilinguals use, for what, and with whom. They need to show students their awareness and interest in their bilingualism. Melissa went to help Herman, a kindergarten child in a mainstream class. Although five, he was characterized as working at the level of a three-year-old. Melissa found out that although English was his strongest language, he used ASL with his deaf mother, and Spanish with his grandparents, with whom he spent every weekend. Melissa, bilingual in English and ASL, started to use both languages in her work with Herman. This child's literacy, as well as classroom behavior, dramatically changed for the better in the four months that Melissa worked with him.

Learning about students' general interests and concerns helps teachers initiate students to literacy or new skills through topics of interest to them and related to their background experience. Seeing Maria writing repeatedly "mamaamaapapa"(mother loves father), the teacher asked her "Y que hay de tu perra?" (what about your dog?). Maria's eyes lit up and she quickly wrote "Yo tenyo una pera negra que se llama Rinse" (I have a black dog called Rinse). Familiarity with the students' experiences also helps teachers find appropriate reading materials, interpret and revise writing, and understand their interpretation of text. Melissa brought a pile of books when using the Reading Aloud approach (see Appendix B) with kindergarten students. By letting the students choose the books, she learned the books they liked and their favorite topics. This led her to bring books of authors the students enjoyed and on topics that sparked their interest.

Bilinguals make use of all their resources in both languages when confronted with a new and difficult task. Familiarity with the students' languages helps teachers to understand their performance. For example, bilingual students interpret the second-language writing system using both their knowledge of the native and second languages. A combination of how they pronounce the word in English with their knowledge of sound–letter correspondence either in English or in their first language play a role in their invented spelling. A Vietnamese child spelled the word *shoe* as *xu,* which is the way that those sounds would be spelled in Vietnamese. A Spanish-speaking child wrote *DN* for The End. He pronounced *the* as *de* and *end* as *en.* Many Spanish speakers have difficulty with the *th* sound and with final consonant clusters. Understanding why these children spell words the way they do helps us realize that they have good decoding skills. All they need to learn are the specific rules of English and how to pronounce English. It is a language and not a literacy issue. The lesson needs to be focused on language and not on literacy skills.

Students use their cultural knowledge to interpret text and create text. This can lead to misinterpretations and inappropriate text organization and use of words when reading and writing in a second language. Knowing the students' culture and how it influences language allows teachers to help students bridge these cultural gaps to reach full literacy proficiency in the new language.

Language attitudes influence learning. Bilinguals and their families benefit from positive attitudes toward both languages. Teachers can help bilinguals achieve this goal. Andrés, a seventh-grade Puerto Rican student, refused to participate in his ESL class. The first entry in his dialogue journal was in Spanish. Assisted by a bilingual colleague, the ESL teacher found out that Andrés felt that Americans did not like him or care about him. He wanted to go back to Puerto Rico. The ESL teacher wrote a short sentence explaining that she did care about him. Andrés' attitude changed radically. He switched to writing his journals in English and slowly began to participate in class.

Teachers who work with many linguistic groups cannot be expected to know about all of the languages and cultures of the students. An awareness of these differences and careful observations of their students can begin to teach them what to expect and why. Traditional explanations given to monolingual speakers of English do not always help bilingual learners. Such is the case of the long–short vowel distinction given to monolinguals when reading words such as *pin/pine* and *cut/cute.* To a bilingual they do not sound as long or short vowels, but as two different sounds. For Spanish-speaking students, the difficulty lies in the vowel sounds of *pin* and *cut,* which don't exist in Spanish.

Often commonly held assumptions do not work with students of other cultures. The teacher wondered why Nestor, a Portuguese student, did not make the association between *Thanksgiving* and *turkey* on a worksheet. Portuguese people serve turkey for Christmas. They have no associations with the traditional American Thanksgiving because it is a totally new concept for them.

It is not an easy task to know all students thoroughly in a class. It is even worse in the case of middle and secondary schools, where teachers work with large numbers of students in one discipline. The task is complicated even more when students' cultural experiences are varied and different from the teacher's own life experience, values, and assumptions.

Teachers do not need to learn all at once the rather lengthy list of important factors affecting bilingual students (see Appendix A). Instead, they can find out systematically about them while engaging students in activities that will help their literacy development.

The approaches recommended in this book allow exploration into the students' minds and lives, because while implementing the approaches, students constantly contribute with their ideas. Students reveal feelings, family situations, difficulties in school, language needs, and even difficulties they may be having in math through dialogue journals. Caroline learned a great deal about her adolescent students through dialogue journals. Vinh, a Vietnamese student, frequently commented on his difficulties in adjusting to life in the United States: "When I come to the United States I really sad because I don't have any friend … " Beatriz revealed a difficult family situation. Vicki discussed her tendency to get angry easily.

Drawing as Prewriting projects, as well as other writing activities, provide a wealth of information about students' lives, families, and their cultures. A Vietnamese kindergarten teacher adapted Drawing as Prewriting to find out more about her students' families and home literacy activities. She asked the students to do their drawings about home activities. The children took their projects home and asked parents or caretakers to write additional comments further explaining their drawings. The teacher found out a lot about family literacy and homework activities, language use, and family life in general. Some parents even stopped by to provide additional information.

Prereading activities that elicit background knowledge and response activities following reading are rich in associations with students' own knowledge and experiences. Sylvia, a fifth-grade bilingual teacher, rolled down the world map to stimulate brainstorming about explorers in preparation for reading about the topic. Timid one-word responses popped here and there until Eduardo, a recent arrival from Guatemala, stood up, walked to the map and gave the class a lesson on Magellan. Eduardo's previous schooling had provided him with knowledge of this aspect of history that most of the other students lacked. Eduardo was ready to read, whereas the rest of the class needed to do a lot more preparation.

Critical Autobiographies is perhaps the approach that informs teachers most about their students, especially as bilingual learners. Ruth, a remedial English reading teacher, learned a lot about Joseph and his family through using the Critical Autobiography approach. Joseph, an American-born first grader of Korean parentage, dictated to Ruth an elaborate story revealing much of his linguistic abilities and cultural background. Joseph was fluent in both languages and could read and write Korean as well, a fact that neither Ruth nor his classroom teacher knew. The parents admitted to being confused as to which language to use at home. They were unsure how to reconcile their desire for English fluency with increasing evidence of Korean language loss in the family. Joseph's autobiography contained numerous references to the contrasting cultures and his desire to fit into both worlds.

Students form their own notions about reading and writing while developing literacy. Conferences held during process writing reveal a great deal about learners. Hank, an ASL/English student, explained his belief that paragraphs were ruled by size while discussing his paper with the teacher. Through discussions and showing Hank examples of paragraphs in books, Lisa helped him realize that paragraphs were tied to meaning.

Another way to learn about students as readers and writers is to interview them and ask them direct questions about these two processes. Terri asked the students in his seventh-grade science class such questions as: What do they read at home? At school? Who helps them and how? What do they like to read? In which language do they prefer to read? What is easy, what is hard to read? How do they choose a reading? What do they do before reading the book? What do they do when they find a word they don't know? and so on, including a number of similar questions with respect to writing.

Through these interviews, Terri found out about these students' and families' literacy habits, their preferences, and strategies. Some students get help from parents, others from siblings, yet others get no help at home. Some write what they are told by the teacher, others prefer to write when they are not ordered to do it. Some glance through the book before starting, others start right away, others check the table of contents.

BILINGUAL–BICULTURAL APPROACH TO TEACHING

Language and culture are central to the development of literacy for bilingual students. Teachers must consider language and culture within the approaches they use, whether the program is bilingual, ESL, mainstream, or foreign language. Students' level of language proficiency should not deter teachers from having high expectations, but it should alert them to provide assistance to reach those expectations.

A bilingual–bicultural approach to teaching implies that teachers, bilingual or not:

- Use both languages for literacy instruction.
- Develop reading and writing simultaneously with speaking and listening skills in the second language.
- Provide functional use of the languages.
- Use students' cultural background as a tool for learning.
- Become cultural brokers.
- Engage homes and communities as partners of literacy development.
- Have high expectations regardless of language proficiency.
- Provide appropriate support.

Use of Both Languages for Literacy Instruction

Literacy instruction takes place in the students' native language, in their second language, or in both.[1] Bilingual learners can benefit from the use of both languages, regardless of the language being used for literacy instruction.

There are pedagogical and psychological reasons for using the native language. Students' native languages provide access to academic content, allow more effective interaction, and are part of the students' overall language and literacy knowledge. Valuing the native languages shows respect for the students and families and gives the languages status in the school. It even helps develop proficiency in the second language.[2] A positive attitude toward the native language of students is particularly important when it is not the language of the larger society. Minority languages are vulnerable to losing status and respect.

Allowing students to function in both languages and in an environment that accepts both cultures is a necessary tool to learn in greater depth about the students. In the case of beginners, they may only label pictures in the second language, whereas they write more extended and informative text in the native language. More advanced students may associate topics with one or the other language and prefer to write about or discuss them in a particular language. Using both languages gives them opportunities to include more topics.

Sometimes students do not take advantage of the knowledge they have in one language to acquire the other. Often they think that their native language is getting in the way of learning the second language and they should repress it. Teachers need to show students how their knowledge of one language can help the development of the other. For example, a bilingual science teacher had written on the board *carnivorous, herbivorous*, and so on. She asked the students to guess what kind of animals they were. Her Spanish-speaking students remained silent. She then pointed at the root of the words and asked them if there were similar words in Spanish. After they realized that *carni* was close to *carne*, the Spanish word for meat, and *herbi* to *hierba*, the Spanish word for hay, herbs, and grass, they reached the correct meaning. Even when languages are totally different, knowledge of concepts supports reading and writing about those concepts in the second language.

Bilingual programs, by definition, provide literacy instruction in both languages. Development of native language literacy insures bilingualism and establishes literacy knowledge that serves as the foundation of literacy in other languages.

Second-language or monolingual programs do not include teaching in the native language in their curriculum. Teachers who use a bilingual–bicultural

---

[1]For a review of the research on the various choices see Lombardo (1979).
[2]Lucas and Katz (1994) describe uses of native languages in high schools with multicultural populations.

approach take advantage of the native language in the process of literacy development of the second language, even if they themselves do not know the language of their students. Teachers keep a library with bilingual dictionaries, books in the native language, and bilingual books. They encourage discussion in the native language while planning or revising writing or when discussing readings. They set up Cross-Age Projects with students who share their native languages. They encourage students to seek help from their families, communities, and bilingual tutors. For example, Toshiko, a preservice teacher fluent in Japanese, helped Yuri with her English literacy while completing her training as an ESL teacher. Yuri, a 9-year-old recent arrival from Japan, withdrew when demanded to read and write in English. Toshiko decided to try a dialogue journal. Initially Yuri wrote in Japanese while Toshiko responded in English, followed by the concept paraphrased in Japanese. For example, in the first entry Yuri wrote in Japanese about the cold weather and the need to use heavy coats. Toshiko responded: "It is really cold. Please take care of your health." Followed by a sentence in Japanese: "It is really cold, isn't it? Please do not catch a cold." By Week 5, Yuri attempted a few English words in her Japanese writing and the teacher responded mostly in English. In Week 7, she wrote a full sentence in English, and in Week 10, she wrote a full story as a class assignment apart from her dialogue journal. Allowing the use of the native language was an effective strategy to change Yuri's attitude toward reading and writing in English.

Holistic Approach to Second-Language Development

Learning the language is an essential component of learning to read and write in a second language. Oral and written language development are best done together to reinforce each other. There is no need to wait for advanced oral language proficiency to start literacy in the second language.[3] Students can be introduced to books and be encouraged to do some writing. Word Cards, Reading Aloud, Shared Reading, and Drawing as Prewriting are some approaches that can be used from the very beginning with the second language. They develop both the written and the oral skills.

There are some students who will be more daring in the written language than the oral because the written language allows time for reflection, correction, and preparation. For example, a seventh-grade Japanese student read a 10 chapter mystery book and wrote summaries in his ESL class with great confidence. He did not dare speak English initially. Oral communication with his teacher, who knew Japanese, was in Japanese. Eventually his success in literacy gave him courage to try English orally.

---

[3]Hudelson (1984) studies the development of literacy in the second language of students with initial oral proficiency.

Functional Use of the Languages

Language serves to communicate ideas. Therefore, the choice of language in the classroom should help in the communication of ideas. Mayra left it up to the student leader to set the choice of language when discussing science topics during Student-Directed Group Discussion. The rest of the students tended to follow the leader using English, Spanish, or codeswitching. The purpose of the activity was to learn science, and to learn to research, present, and write ideas. Either language would serve that purpose.

Language use enhances language proficiency. To motivate students to use a particular language, the teacher must create the circumstances for students to have to use the language. In the Mailbox Game approach described earlier, English-speakers were motivated to write in Spanish when communicating with native Spanish-speakers. Cheryl used the Jigsaw approach for readings in her ESL class to encourage quiet students to talk. Each expert group studied one third of the story well. Then groups were formed with students who had each read part of the story in order to piece it together. A Japanese student admitted that it was so much harder to make herself understood to other students than to the teacher. Her group needed her to be thorough and clear because her piece was important for understanding the whole reading. She was stressed but grateful for the opportunity to have to use the language for real communication.

Children have a very pragmatic view of the choice of languages. Basically they will use the language that the interlocutor knows. It is hard to induce children to use a particular language in order to learn it. Therefore, if the goal is to develop a particular language, students need to be provided with authentic opportunities where they must use that language, and preferably in a friendly and relaxed context. Some students in Peggy's bilingual class choose to function mostly in Spanish, their stronger language. They can, however, use English when dealing with monolingual people. For example, Peggy's sister, who only speaks English, assisted these third graders with their science fair projects. All students participated actively. Yadira wrote a thank-you letter to the visitor. It was her first attempt at writing in English. She wrote:

> Dear Ms. Eileen:
> You are a good helper. Thank you for the candys an the pencils I am glad of you.
> Becuase you are so good for the pizza
> Thank you you are a good helper
> Sincerely,
> Yadira

Cultural Background As a Tool for Learning

Cultural background shapes students' prior knowledge. Prior knowledge, together with language proficiency and literacy ability, holds the key to reading comprehension and development of topic for writing. Teachers can take advantage of prior knowledge to motivate students to read and write and facilitate the process when students are developing language and literacy ability. Giving students choice of topic for their writings stimulates prior knowledge.

When initiating students to second-language reading, teachers can use books in the second language that have culturally familiar themes. For example, the book *Paper Crane* that Peggy used for Shared Reading contains a theme very familiar to Chinese students. The book *Everybody Cooks Rice* illustrates how different cultures use rice in their diet. The book *My First American Friend* by Sarunna Jin tells a story of a Chinese girl who moves to Boston from China. It addresses the theme of making friends in a new environment, an extremely relevant topic for immigrant students.

Using students' prior knowledge enhances motivation to read and write. Students are excited to read books that raise familiar topics and they write endlessly about topics close to them. Education is also about expanding this knowledge. Teachers need to introduce students to reading and writing about unknown topics. To enhance reading comprehension and the quality of composing, teachers must develop students' knowledge in preparation to read or write something. For example, in preparation for writing in his seventh-grade bilingual science class, Terry always had students do a hands-on activity, discuss pictures, or go on a field trip related to the topic, followed by creating a semantic map to discuss the topic, organize the subthemes, and develop vocabulary. Only then did the students write.

Even more effective is to relate newly learned concepts to the students' experience. For example, Peggy asked a group of American-born students of Dominican background about their feelings toward the Dominican Republic, whether they felt they were American or Dominican, and whether their relatives in the Dominican Republic truly understood their lives in the United States. Following a lively discussion, Peggy introduced the parallel situation of the American colonists, their feelings toward England, as well as King George III's apparent lack of understanding of the colonists' point of view.

Teachers As Cultural Brokers

Regardless of the linguistic and cultural background and the specific assignment, teachers working with bilingual students must help them and their families understand and function within the school and the larger society. Teachers' roles as literacy instructors extends to helping students adjust to the new culture and teaching them how to use the language and literacy skills they are developing effectively in the new society. Teachers need to teach the function of literacy, the cultural knowledge needed to comprehend text, the specific meaning of words beyond the literal definitions contained in dictionaries, and the structure of text particular to the new culture.

Different cultures use printed text for different purposes. For example, in many countries newspapers are rather thin and contain mostly news, whereas in the United States they serve multiple purposes. People read the newspapers not only for news but to decide on entertainment, sales, car shopping, and much more. In the United States information is frequently disseminated through printed text. Everywhere we go there is a brochure to read about a particular institution. Directions are always given in writing. This extended use of print can be overwhelming for learners from cultures where oral communication is the norm. When presenting an authentic text, teachers should do it in a complete cultural context. A mainstream teacher regularly wrote the two lunch selections on the board for the benefit of her bilingual students. This way they could learn the vocabulary. Students checked under their choice as they came in. Miguel, a recent arrival from Mexico, not only needed to be taught the menu choices but the whole concept of schools serving lunch and having a choice. In his country students do not eat lunch at school but go home in the early afternoon to have the main meal of the day.[4]

World knowledge and the meaning of words in the cultural context is essential to comprehend text. Students reading text written by an author of a different culture may have difficulty understanding unless teachers give students the background they need. As illustrated in the Vocabulary Connections approach, seventh graders from Latin America interpreted the word *plantation* as a piece of agricultural land. They were reading about the Civil War in the United States. The teacher had to explain the social and historical meaning of plantations in the South. Students quickly understood and related it to comparable situations in Latin America.

Teachers must also explain the organization and content of text depending on the genre. For example, a persuasive essay is a foreign concept to American Indians[5] who believe in presenting both sides of the argument for a reader to decide.[6] Even grammar can be culturally defined. Eskimos use the modal *would* to soften an assertion. " ... the stories are going down generations of natives to the younger generations so the customs *wouldn't* be forgotten."[7] Using *would* is preferable to *will* because there is no certainty that it will happen. This is consistent with Eskimo talk that requires circumspection.

Teachers as cultural brokers build a bridge between the students and the intended meaning of the author when reading, and between students and their audience when writing. Comparing, contrasting, and finding similar circumstances in the students' culture help.

---

[4]Heath (1986) discusses the need to focus on context when teaching literacy to students who experience a new language and culture.

[5]We followed the recommendation of McCarty and Watahomigie (1998) in our choice of the term "American Indian" to refer to indigenous groups in the United States.

[6]Conklin and Lourie (1983, chap. 11) and Connor and Kaplan (1987) address the cultural differences among languages.

[7]Basham and Kwachka (1991, p. 41).

Homes and Communities As Partners
of Literacy Development

Teachers and parents contribute to the literacy experience of students, complementing and reinforcing each other. In the case of bilingual students, they also collectively contribute to the students' full linguistic development. Neither can do it alone, but together they can build a strong foundation. Bilingual learners need development of both languages, of social as well as academic literacy skills, and of knowledge to support literacy in English. Language proficiency, educational background, and views of literacy learning determine what teachers and parents can offer to the students. For example, the school may not be able to provide instruction in the native language, but the family can. Teachers should then encourage the family to strengthen the native language including literacy rather than, as often happens, press them to switch to English. It is better to let the school take care of the English, but both can support the work that the other is doing.

Schools that offer bilingual literacy still benefit from any help the parents give their children. Homes have many opportunities to provide rich literacy experiences in either language. The key is maintaining a proper balance and reinforcing the notion that both languages are important. Constant and trusting communication between parents and teachers can help establish what each can offer and how each can reinforce the work of the other. Melissa had been using Reading Aloud in English with Herman, a trilingual English, Spanish, and ASL hearing child of a deaf mother. Three months into the project, Melissa invited Herman's mother to join them. Herman was embarrassed and hesitant to sign the stories to his mother. With his mother's encouragement he gained confidence and read her several books, signing the text in ASL. After he was finished, the mother taught him signs he did not know for animals and pictures in the books. This activity changed the mother's negative perceptions of her son's interest in books and general behavior. She decided to start reading with him at home, using the books that she had kept on the top shelf of a closet out of his reach.

When neither parents nor teachers can provide skills, community resources should be tapped. A productive resource is tutors from neighboring colleges, especially those who are in teacher preparation programs specifically geared to bilingual learners. These tutors are supervised and have developed useful background on how to work with bilingual students. Tutors' work needs to be closely coordinated with classroom teachers. Sylvia, an ESL major, was in charge of helping a seventh-grade Russian student in a mainstream classroom. She consulted with his teacher and found out that he needed particular help with summaries of his readings. The reading assignment was about Thomas Edison. Following the Reader-Generated Questions approach, she asked Steve to imagine what his friends would like to know about Edison and formulate some questions. Steve asked: When did Edison invent the phonograph? How did he get the idea? How did he make it? How does it work? Why did he invent it? What other things did he invent? Sylvia copied down the questions and put them aside while Steve read the excerpt on Edison. Then she asked Steve to write down answers to his questions based on the reading. Using a process approach to writing, they turned the list of answers into a summary of the reading. This was an elaborate process that required a one-to-one approach quite appropriate for a tutor and extremely helpful for Steve's participation in his class.

High Expectations

Language development, educational experience, and difficult life circumstances make the task of teaching many bilingual students challenging, but should not act as a deterrent to having high expectations for such students. These expectations must be backed by support provided to the students so that they can reach these goals.

Approaches recommended in this book allow students to control the level of difficulty. Regardless of ability, all students should be required to participate to the extent that they can. For example, Chiet, a recent arrival from China in a mainstream kindergarten, was able to participate alongside her classmates in the Word Card activity because all she needed to bring was a new word every day. Serious personal circumstances had delayed Nestor's cognitive development, yet he could participate as well as the other students by using the Drawing as Prewriting approach. He drew elaborate pictures and then dictated the story to his teacher. It took several months before Nestor started writing his own short sentences. Other students in the class could write on their own after drawing, yet others were beyond needing to compose first through drawings and could write directly, illustrating later. All the students in the class produced books, yet each worked to his or her own individual potential.

Appropriate Support

Sometimes the demands of the curriculum are difficult because of language, cultural content, or limited education. Teachers should not waiver in their expectations, but they should find ways to provide the appropriate support. Strategies that help students reach curriculum goals are helpful to all students. They are, however, essential for bilingual learners, especially when instruction is in their second language. For example, José, a high school student with fluency in English, found the social studies book difficult. Lisa used the KWL approach (see Appendix B) to help him cope with the content. They filled the columns "K" for all he knew about the subject and "W" for all he wanted to learn about the topic. He read the selection and then filled the "L" column with all he had learned after reading. During the discussion that accompanied filling out the first two columns Lisa was able to clarify vocabulary, concepts, misconceptions, and most important, the lack of prior knowledge that José had on the subject.

Other helpful strategies are:

- Providing direct instruction.
- Modeling tasks.
- Facilitating transitions.
- Providing practice opportunities.
- Providing corrective feedback.
- Becoming a partner in the reading and writing process.
- Organizing the classroom into flexible groups.
- Using homework as a preparation to function in class.
- Allowing extra time to complete tasks.
- Teaching vocabulary before reading or writing.
- Using the computer.

Direct Instruction.   Teachers show students exactly the process they need to go through to achieve what they want. They practice with the students and continue giving support until they can do it independently. For example, Tricia, working with a group of ESL high school students, carefully taught them how to write summaries. She used Graphic Organizers, KWL, predicting, and looking for the main idea to enhance reading comprehension of passages. Then she taught students to look for things they did not understand, for the main idea, and for important and unimportant details. She insisted that students use their own words. The focus on the main idea and modeling the process helped students improve their summary writing and eliminated the practice of copying from the original text.[8]

Direct instruction avoids frustration, especially when students are in the early stages of developing a second language. Alma's students had read a story in English and were now discussing it in Bosnian. They were assigned to write a summary in English. While her students were discussing, Alma listened to their conversation and noted key words that she felt would be needed for the summary. She then taught the students how to say and write those words in English while they put together a story map. The students not only used those words when writing the summary, but used them appropriately in other writings later on. In the past, students were frustrated because they could discuss the story in Bosnian, but did not have the words to then write about it in English.

Modeling.   Teachers demonstrate to students what they are requested to do by carrying out the activity while thinking aloud. Often students may not follow instructions either because they are given in their weaker language or because they are unfamiliar with what the teacher wants them to do. School tasks that may seem routine to teachers are often very strange to children be-

---

[8]Prinz (1998) contains a full account of this project.

cause they were neither part of their previous schooling nor used at home. Modeling helps students understand what they are expected to do. Linda introduced Drawing as Prewriting to her deaf students by drawing pictures while signing her thoughts. She pondered what to draw, what crayons to choose, what to add in the picture, and what to write down. The children watched her carefully and soon started to imitate. Some, of course, even copied her picture but eventually would draw their own.

Facilitating Transition.   Teachers need to allow time and support students when they are not used to a particular approach. Sarah used Process Writing with her high school ESL students. Horacio refused to plan before writing. He was an intelligent and well-read young man who could write on complex topics. When it was time for writing he would start right away and produce several pages. His writings looked disorganized to his teacher, often going off on tangents. After three weeks of working with him, Sarah finally succeeded in having him brainstorm on a topic of interest. He then chose one aspect of it and together they created a semantic map while they discussed the topic in more depth. The resulting essay was clear, organized, and well developed. Both teacher and student were pleased with the results. Sarah's perseverance, patience, and flexibility paid off.

Some approaches require students to do something totally different from the expected classroom behavior. Students appear confused either because of the innovative nature of the approaches, or the fact that they were not used in the country where they initiated their schooling. Elena decided to use Reader-Generated Questions in her sixth-grade social studies class. When she asked students to formulate questions prior to reading, the students refused, claiming that only teachers asked questions. It took Elena the whole 45-minute period to eradicate a belief that had been established after several years of traditional schooling where teachers lecture and ask questions while students listen and respond.

Practice.   Rehearsing and repetition help retain language skills. This practice does not have to be tedious and boring. Poems, songs, and games are helpful ways to work with language. For example, Yoko used a game to practice vocabulary and sound–letter correspondence with her ESL students. She said the first word and then the students took turns saying words that started with the last letter of the previous word. For example: *kangaroo - October - rabbit - Tuesday*, and so on. To assist her learners, she wrote the words on the board so that they could clearly see the last letter of the word.

After collecting a number of words through the Word Card activity, Kim developed a board game for her second-grade Vietnamese students who were learning English. She drew a start to finish winding trail. In some boxes she wrote words, and in others she drew the equivalent pictures. Groups of students took turns, putting their pieces in the start box. The student who won the first turn moved his piece to the first square with the word *squirrel*. Without hesitation, he jumped to the square with the picture of the squirrel. When students could not guess which was the corresponding picture or word, or they guessed wrong, they just moved to the next square. Thus, the more words they knew, the faster they could move.

Corrective Feedback. There is a delicate balance between promoting language accuracy and discouraging students with correction. Constant correction interrupts the thinking process and overtaxes short-term memory. On the other hand, students developing a language need feedback to approach accuracy. In the case of bilingual learners with varied input in each language, teachers cannot be sure that the natural environment is going to provide appropriate models for the students to learn naturally. Therefore, some measure of corrective feedback is necessary. Jin was doing Drawing as Prewriting in English with her second-grade Chinese students. Brandon insisted on doing the writing himself. Jin encouraged him to sound out words every time he requested spelling assistance. In addition, she would help with selected words. For example, after sounding out *caught*, he wrote *caut*. Jin told him to add a *g* after *au*. He added *gh*, arriving at the correct spelling. He only needed some encouragement to help him remember how to spell the word.

Teacher as a Partner in the Reading and Writing Process.
Teachers can facilitate the reading and writing process by intervening where the students are having difficulty. Reading aloud with expression, writing down what the students try to compose, sounding out words for spelling, and reading aloud to revise a piece are among the types of intervention that efficiently assist students.

Reading aloud with expression (see Appendix B) while students listen greatly enhances reading comprehension and the development of knowledge of text structure. When students can follow along with the text, it enhances the acquisition of sound–letter correspondence. Even students who are fluent in oral language profit from listening to a good reader. June, a mainstream social studies teacher, read aloud test items for the benefit of her bilingual students.

Writing down what students dictate takes the stress off beginning writers in their second language. Reiko's student dictated the sentences for her initial drawings during the Drawing as Prewriting approach. After the first few sessions, the student ventured to write by herself such sentences as "This is Boston Common," "Fish is many." A first-grade teacher sat at a computer with a student who refused to write. The student dictated the first sentence; the teacher encouraged him to write the next. Together they wrote a whole page story alternating typing the sentences. When the page was printed the student took full credit for the story. He also continued to write on his own after that session.

Sounding out words to the students can help them spell. For example, Brandon wanted to write the word *gigantic*, but he couldn't spell it and couldn't sound it out. Jin sounded it out for him and he was able to spell it correctly. Leo, a Spanish as a second language teacher, used Semantic Maps and Process Writing with his high school students. During revision he would read aloud a student's piece. Students themselves found incongruencies and mistakes while Leo read.

Flexible Grouping.[9]   All students' needs can be best met when the class is organized in various types of grouping from whole class, to small groups, to pairs or individuals working by themselves. Students can be grouped in teams of comparable abilities, similar interests, specific language or literacy needs, or heterogeneously. Group variation allows for development of different strengths and needs. No student should be kept in the same group all the time. Students, especially at the secondary level, may resist working in groups because they come from a schooling experience where there was no such practice. Teachers need to be sensitive to these cultural differences and develop strategies to help students work together and see the value of this cooperation. Pauline, an English-speaking music teacher, had a number of Chinese bilingual students in her class, including two new arrivals who spoke only Chinese. She divided her 40 students into groups of five. Each group included English speakers, Chinese students fluent in both languages, and those with more limited proficiency in English. Using both languages, students communicated and created final drafts in English of American composers for inclusion in the class anthology. All students, regardless of language ability, contributed to the group's product. Close work with English speakers in the small groups helped Chinese students gain confidence to later actively participate in the oral presentation of their projects in front of the whole class.

Homework.   Teachers should assign homework to prepare students to function in class the following day rather than to finish what they did not get around to doing in class. For the Vocabulary Connections approach, homework can be looking up the assigned words in the dictionary and writing down the definitions, so that the following day the teacher can concentrate on the discussion about the words. For Process Writing, it can be thinking about the topic they want to write about, doing a Semantic Map, and reading about it, so that when they come to class they can start working on the draft or discussing what they will write. For Word Cards, students can think of the word or words they will bring for the activity and drawing a picture that represents the word, so when they come to class they can tell the word and show their picture. For Jig-

---

[9]See Radencich and McKay (1995) for explanation and examples of the use of flexible grouping in a variety of classroom contexts.

saw, the expert group can do research on their piece of the puzzle. ESL and mainstream teachers can have students read in the native language or ask adults at home about topics that they will read or write in class in English.

When homework is to prepare students for class as suggested here, then any help that they get at home is useful. When homework is just worksheet or workbook tasks, having adults do them for the children defeats the purpose of the assignment.

Extra Time.   Students who are working in the second language or have difficulty with their native language, can profit from extra time to get their task accomplished. Steve, a seventh-grade Russian student, never wanted to revise his work. He felt under pressure to hand in the work. He expected the teacher to make the corrections. When the teacher implemented process writing to help him produce his science papers and allowed him extra time before handing in the papers, he was more willing to make revisions.

Vocabulary Development.   Vocabulary can be a big block in reading comprehension and expression in writing. There are number of ways to develop the vocabulary such as the Vocabulary Connections approach, Word Cards, Semantic Mapping, providing words when doing Drawing as Prewriting, or through Dialogue Journal.

Yoko chose key words from the readings she was using for the Reader-Generated Question approach. She wrote them on index cards, discussed them with the student before the student generated the questions, and gave him the cards to keep. Teaching the vocabulary facilitated reading comprehension. The student also used these words in the final summaries of the stories.

Cristina set out to try the Framework on Critical Literacy approach (see Appendix B). She never went beyond the second step because her student was intent on learning every word in the reading. Initially she explained or sometimes translated the word; other times she related it to the student's experience or to a cognate in Spanish, the student's native language. Eventually she encouraged the student to figure out the meaning from the context.

Use of the Computer.   Word processing, spell checkers, reading and content area programs, language practice exercises, and Internet access provide support for literacy development. The word processor motivates students because it takes away the drudgery of using paper and pencil and revising drafts. The final product is a lot neater. "I feel writing on the Word Processor is easier and faster. Another thing is that it is easier to make neat because you don't have to worry about eraser marks" (sixth grader).

Good quality software can provide meaningful opportunities to read and write. There are stories with interactive features, and in some cases, in a variety of languages that provide good reading and language practice. Other software programs as well as the Internet motivate students to read in order to do research. It is important to be flexible. Debbie, a Spanish as a second language high school teacher, allowed her students to choose the type of program in which they wanted to work. Some students chose word processing, database, and other creative programs, whereas others preferred drill and practice programs that allowed them to build confidence in the language. Eventually, these students used word processing to do creative writing.

E-mail has been widely used to connect one group of students with students in other places allowing them to practice reading and writing skills in different languages. This type of interaction makes students truly aware of the need to use appropriate and comprehensible language because they need to be understood and it is very public. It also motivates students to use both their languages through a real need to communicate.[10] Debbie registered Spanish as a second language classes with the global satellite telecommunications project *Orilla a Orilla*.[11] Debbie's class was paired with a class in Chile. Her students wrote letters in Spanish introducing themselves and e-mailed them to Chile. They also prepared a box of gifts to send to Chile. Students brought gifts and wrote why these objects were important to them. Next they carried out a project about Chile. They e-mailed questions to their Chilean partners to seek assistance with their research project. Other cooperatively developed projects followed. According to Debbie, the students were highly motivated to use the language and greatly improved their Spanish.[12]

USING INSTRUCTION FOR ASSESSMENT

Assessment is a vital component of every classroom. Teachers assess their students to aid in the planning, carrying out, and altering of classroom instruction for one, some, or all the students. Teachers constantly monitor their students' learning to assure that the intended instructional goals are being met. Through daily observation, questioning, and written evaluations teachers determine the effectiveness of a lesson or approach to learning; and decide if, when, and how to change the approach to assure that all students learn.

When assessment in the classroom is coordinated with instruction, it provides a productive, meaningful, and fair way of improving teaching and enhancing learning.[13] Assessment procedures should become an integral part of teachers' lesson planning. In this way, instruction informs assessment, and vice versa. Instead of waiting until the end of a unit to assess what and how much was learned by the students, ongoing, integrated assessment provides immedi-

---

[10]Cummins and Sayers (1995) wrote about the power of computers and Internet communication.

[11]The program's web page address is *http://orillas.upr.clu.edu/*. The e-mail address is <*orillas-info@igc.org*>

[12]Isom (1995).

[13]See Brisk (1998a) for a discussion of the benefits of planning instruction in conjunction with assessment and Stefanakis (1998) for examples of teachers carrying out this practice.

ate feedback to both students and teachers. Any needed changes in instruction and direction can occur at the most opportune time, during the learning itself.

The act of becoming literate is both ongoing and developmental. Therefore, assessments for bilingual students should focus on the process as well as the product. It is often during the process of reading and writing that one observes students using, improving, and eventually mastering literacy skills and techniques.

The process of literacy assessment in the classroom is multidimensional, and includes assessing knowledge of content, knowledge of text structure, vocabulary, grammar, orthography, and sound–symbol correspondence. It is important for teachers to determine the processes and skills the students have mastered, those that need reinforcement, and those that need to be taught, or retaught.

For bilingual students, assessment should be performed in both the first and second language because many literacy skills are not language specific. Students demonstrate literacy knowledge through either language, whereas they demonstrate ability to read and write in a particular language through that specific language. Students can demonstrate the ability to encode words through either their first or second language; however, demonstrating the correct spelling of a word is done in the language in question.

By assessing in either language, teachers can ascertain the students' ability to read and write various genre, how well students manipulate aspects of language in context, as well as how students understand content-specific material. Assessing in both languages will also provide the teacher better information as to the developmental level of literacy of the students. Students can best demonstrate what they know and what they have learned when they are given the opportunity to relate it to prior knowledge and experience. For bilinguals, that prior knowledge and experience may be in the first language.

Teachers who are not speakers of the students' other language should find ways to evaluate students' performance in that other language. Alicia, a monolingual English teacher, asked Angela, a bilingual colleague, to assess José's reading ability in Spanish. Angela heard José read aloud and checked for comprehension while Alicia watched. They were both able to see that José had limited Spanish reading skills. Further talks with the mother confirmed that she did not encourage José's Spanish development.

There are also occasions when both languages can be utilized for one assessment. Students, who may be able to read and understand a passage in the second language, but cannot produce a written summary in the second language, would better demonstrate understanding of what was read if given the opportunity to write the summary in their native language. Again, translation assistance can be asked of teachers, paraprofessionals, other students, and parents if the teacher is not proficient in the first language of the student.

When assessing a bilingual student's performance, teachers must also be aware of the effect culture and background knowledge have on student responses and reactions. A more complete picture of students' literacy experience and knowledge is obtained when teachers have an understanding of how much students' answers are dependent on their first language and culture. When asked for the identity of the character, as the teacher pointed to the hen (in *The Little Red Hen* story), one girl exclaimed: "The mother." In her culture, a female wearing an apron always represents the mother. Teachers need to investigate further when students give a seemingly incorrect answer.

Assessment Practices

Teachers need to decide exactly what will be assessed, how and when they will assess students, how the information will be recorded, and how feedback will be given to the students and, when appropriate, to the parents or other members of the school community.

The decision on what will be assessed should be made during the planning stages of the lesson, so that instruction and assessment complement each other. Once teachers determine which aspects of literacy development will be assessed, they will need to select a method of assessment. There are a number of highly recommended assessment practices such as oral interviews, read alouds, retellings, writing samples, experiments and demonstrations, projects and exhibitions, response journals, learning logs, constructed responses, and conferences. (See Appendix D for description of these practices.[14]) Many of these assessment practices are embedded in the approaches recommended in this book (see Table 5.1).

Patricia, a mainstream computer teacher, experimented with Process Writing with her class of fifth graders. She used read alouds during revision, collected writing samples, and carried out conferences with individual students. All these activities provided rich information on her students' writing ability with respect to both process and product. She noticed that several Spanish speakers' first drafts lacked some articles. One student wrote: "When I was baby ... " Another wrote: "What I think of me being Scorpio is ... " When the students read aloud, however, they included the missing article and later corrected the error while producing their final version.

Teachers must plan assessment of both process and product. By observing, talking to the students, and taking notes during a lesson or activity teachers are able to see more clearly how well students are progressing, or if parts of a lesson or concept have been misunderstood or forgotten by the students. Observations and questioning of the students during a lesson or activity may help prevent an incorrect assessment of students' ability.[15] Tests, as well as demonstrations, exhibitions, projects, experiments, and writing samples, are means of assessing a product. Bilingual students do need to learn the traditional method

---

[14]Genesee and Hamayan (1994) and O'Malley and Valdez-Pierce (1996) explain in detail these practices.

[15]See Farr and Trumbull (1997) for a more detailed explanation of process assessment.

TABLE 5.1
Assessment Practices That Can Be Used With the Approaches

	Oral Interviews	Read Alouds	Re-tellings	Writing Samples	Projects Exhibitions	Experiments	Response Journals	Learning Logs	Constructed Responses	Conferences
1 Cooperative Learning–Jigsaw	X		X		X	X		X	X	X
2 Critical Autobiography	X				X				X	X
3 Cross-Age Project	X	X				X		X		
4 Dialogue Journal	X		X	X					X	
5 Drawing as Prewriting	X			X					X	
6 Graph Org – Semantic Mapping	X									X
7 Language Experience Approach	X	X		X						X
8 Mailbox Game	X			X						
9 Process Writing	X	X		X						X
10 Process Writing with Computers	X			X					X	
11 Reader-Generated Questions	X	X	X			X	X		X	X
12 Response to Literature	X		X	X	X		X		X	X
13 Show Not Tell	X			X						X
14 Shared Reading	X	X							X	
15 Sharing Time/Group Discussion	X				X	X	X	X	X	
16 Talk–Write										
17 Vocabulary Connection	X			X			X	X	X	
18 Word Cards	X	X								X

of question and answer, multiple choice, and true–false type evaluations, because it does assess declarative knowledge of a subject,[16] and it is the more common type of assessment in many classrooms, not to mention the more formal standardized tests. However, assessments involving exhibitions, projects, or demonstrations can give teachers a broader perspective both on what the students learned as well as how the student was able to apply what was learned. Students in a bilingual third-grade class were studying about different communities (i.e., urban, suburban, and rural). As a culminating project, the students worked in cooperative groups and designed the type of community they would like to live in. Students worked together to decide the types of buildings and services their community would have. When the projects were finished, mainstream teachers were invited into the classroom to question individual students on components of their project. It was each student's responsibility to know the community well enough to answer any question asked. Gene, the classroom teacher, observed while the students were being questioned and made notes of how well each student was able to explain the project.

Information emerging from the assessment activities can be recorded with the assistance of checklists; narrative, anecdotal, and running records; video and audio recordings; and portfolios. These descriptive records enable teachers to show in some detail the progress a student is making. Bilingual and ESL teachers, for example, can use this type of assessment and recording when consulting with other teachers or administrators to decide whether a student is ready to be mainstreamed into an all English curriculum. On the other hand, a portfolio, containing selected samples of students' work in all subject areas, gives parents a comprehensive overview of what their child is learning and how their child is performing in the classroom.

Putting it all Together: Approaches As Assessment Tools

There are innumerable opportunities during the implementation of the approaches recommended in this handbook for teachers to assess the literacy development and specific skills acquisition of their students. One approach can be used in several ways to evaluate literacy development and skills. As mentioned previously, teachers should have a clear understanding of what, why and how they are assessing before proceeding (i.e., which literacy skills do they want to assess and for what purposes).

Table 5.2 shows examples of skills[17] that can be taught and assessed through the Reader-Generated Question approach and where in the process of the approach the skill is demonstrated.

---

[16]See Marzano, Pickering, and Tighe (1993) for assessment standards for declarative and procedural knowledge.

[17]Many of these skills are listed in literacy record folders used by many public school systems.

TABLE 5.2
Literacy Skills Assessed Through Reader-Generated
Question Approach

Reading Skills Assessed	Where in the Approach
Uses context cues	Step 4: Presentation of text
	Step 5: Checking out responses
Uses knowledge of language structure	Step 2: Generation of questions
	Step 3: Responding to questions
Predicts	Step 1: Stimuli
	Step 4: Presentation of text
Rereads to establish meaning	Step 4: Presentation of text
	Step 5: Checking out responses
Reads further to gain more information	Step 5: Checking out responses
Self-corrects	Step 2: Generation of questions
	Step 3: Responding to questions
	Step 4: Presentation of text
Uses picture cues to establish meaning	Step 1: Stimuli
	Step 4: Presentation of text
States main idea of paragraph	Step 6: Final activity
Gives details to support the main idea	Step 6: Final activity
Infers meaning from text	Step 5: Checking out responses
	Step 6: Final activity
Expresses and supports an opinion	Step 3: Responding to questions
	Step 6: Final activity
Uses a range of books and other materials to locate information	Step 5: Checking out responses

Writing Skills Assessed	Where in the Approach
Interprets maps, graphs, and tables in context	Step 4: Presentation of text
	Step 5: Checking out responses
Skims a paragraph to find relevant information	Step 4: Presentation of text
	Step 5: Checking out responses
Compares and contrasts information	Step 4: Presentation of text
	Step 5: Checking out responses
	Step 6: Final activity
Draws conclusion	Step 6: Final activity

continued on following page

Writing Skills Assessed	Where in the Approach
Writes comprehensible sentences	Step 2: Generation of questions
	Step 3: Responding to questions
	Step 6: Final activity
Stays on the topic of writing	Step 6: Final activity
Connects ideas	Step 2: Generation of questions
	Step 3: Responding to questions
	Step 5: Checking out responses
	Step 6: Final activity
Is aware of audience	Step 6: Final activity
Uses compound sentences	Step 3: Responding to questions
	Step 6: Final activity
Uses content-specific vocabulary	Step 2: Generation of questions
	Step 3: Responding to questions
	Step 6: Final activity
Uses correct punctuation	Step 2: Generation of questions
	Step 3: Responding to questions
	Step 6: Final activity
Uses invented spelling	Step 2: Generation of questions
	Step 3: Responding to questions
	Step 6: Final activity
Uses conventional spelling	Step 2: Generation of questions
	Step 3: Responding to questions
	Step 6: Final activity
Revises work	Step 6: Final activity
Edits work	Step 6: Final activity
Uses dictionary, thesaurus, and so forth to increase vocabulary and understanding	Step 5: Checking out responses
	Step 6: Final activity
Uses standard grammar	Step 2: Generation of questions
	Step 3: Responding to questions
	Step 6: Final activity

Renate (see the Reader-Generated Question approach) was able to assess many of the skills listed previously for the children with whom she was working. Often during the Generation of Questions and Responding to Questions steps of the process, the children self-corrected their remarks. For example, George had begun a response to a question about plants by saying, "Cause ... ", but corrected it to *because* as Renate was beginning to write it down. Angel also rephrased a question he had about plants and energy to make it more explicit. He had first asked: "Why do plants like energy, energy?," but then changed it to: "Why do trees need the light energy?" Renate was also able to determine which students needed reinforcement in the formation of questions in English. In addition, she noticed during the Checking Out Responses step, that the students seemed more comfortable writing the answers directly from the text instead of rephrasing. From this observation, she realized that the students needed to practice extracting information from text and writing it in their own words. During the reading of the text, in an effort to find answers to their questions about plants, students reread paragraphs and discussed the main points of them. At other times, when the information was not available in the textbooks, the students had to use other sources of information to find answers to their questions. Renate was able to see which students knew how to use sources such as other science texts, science information books, and encyclopedias.

Clearly, a teacher would not want to assess all the skills a particular approach allows. The purpose of the checklist is to show the numerous skills that can be assessed by using one of the approaches. Teachers can adapt the list depending on what they have decided to assess. When using a checklist, teachers should indicate whether students were able to complete the skill independently, with assistance, or not at all.

For example, a teacher might want to create a checklist similar to the one shown in Table 5.3. Teachers should indicate how well the student can perform a task by circling the appropriate letter. Write the date of the observation on the line next to the letter. Indicate the language in which the skill is observed.

TABLE 5.3
Sample Checklist

Student Name	Uses Context Cues	Predicts	Infers Meaning
	I____H____N____*	I____H____N____	I____H____N____
	I____H____N____	I____H____N____	I____H____N____
	I____H____N____	I____H____N____	I____H____N____
	I____H____N____	I____H____N____	I____H____N____

*I = Can do Independently; H = Can do with help; N = Cannot do at all.

Observations and anecdotal records are helpful when teachers want to track the development of certain skills of the students. Susan (see Drawing as Prewriting approach) was able to observe developmental changes in Alex's ability to decode the words he had written. In the beginning of her study, Susan had noted that Alex demonstrated great difficulty in reading the stories he had written. Later on, she observed that he was able to read some of the sentences he had written, but not many. Eventually, Susan observed that Alex was able to completely read his story aloud to his classmates. An example of her anecdotal record follows:

February 12, 1993
When I had Alex read me his story, he couldn't remember what it said. We went through it very slowly together and tried sounding out the words. Alex did not know the sounds of most of the letters and when I gave them to him, he had difficulty putting them together. We read the story three times together, and by the third time it was better, but he still did not know all of the words. When he showed his teacher, he made no attempt to read it and she read it to him.

Later on, Susan observed that Alex was able to read more of the sentences he had written:

February 26, 1993
... Alex was able to read aloud what he had dictated to me, which he could not do last week.

During the course of her time with Alex, Susan noticed that he was remembering the sound–symbol correspondence of many consonants:

March 4, 1993
Alex recognized graphophonemic correspondences for *s, d, f, l, t,* and *v.* He had some difficulty with vowel sounds, but even then he knew they were vowel sounds. He also knew that the letters *k* and *c* can sound alike.

Eventually, Susan observed that Alex was able to confidently read his story aloud to his classmates:

April 6, 1993
Alex read last. Saroeut and Elvin had stood up and were talking and Alex hit Saroeut in the knee with his paper. "Sit down!" he said and they did. When Alex read, all of the students moved in very close so that they could hear him better. While some of the other students read, there were people kind of shuffling around and looking around. When Alex read, they all practically sat on top of him and everyone wanted to help him read. He read his story very well and the few places he got stuck, Saroeut helped him with the words.

While using the LEA with Teddy, Laurie was able to observe the progress he made decoding words in a story. She writes:

March 21, 1996
I told Teddy to read one sentence at a time and I would write it on the sentence strip. Teddy read the first four sentences with accuracy and fluency. He had difficulty with the word *figured* in his next sentence. He identified the initial sound and used the long i vowel sound. He then made a guess *fired*, based on these first two sounds and looked at me. I said, "Let's skip over that word and read the rest of the sentence. This may remind you of what you said." He was able to read the rest of the sentence and then exclaimed, "Oh, yah! Figured." as he went back to the beginning of the sentence. In the next sentence he struggled with the word *friends*. Again he identified the two initial sounds and made an attempt at the word, coming up with freed. With a single cue to recall his story he readily came to the conclusion that the word was friends. When *friends* reappeared in the next sentence he had no difficulty recalling it.

March 26, 1996
At the beginning of our third session I asked Teddy to continue to read his dictated text, … He was able to read "Please ostrich play with me." He self-corrected when he began to read *play* as *please…* Teddy at times will confuse *b* and *d* as he did in the next sentence, as he attempted to decode *didn't* with the /b/ sound. He realized his own error because he self-corrected without any cues.

April 29, 1996
… Teddy was able to read the first twelve pages of the original *Milton the Early Riser*. His reading was quite fluent, in that he was able to recognize many of the words by sight. He read seven of the twelve pages without any errors … Teddy applied his decoding skills when he reached *trembled*. He omitted the /r/ sound in his initial attempt, on he second attempt he went back over the sounds and said all of them. However, he guessed the word to be troubled. I cued him to try it again. I assisted him by covering up some of the phonemes as he proceeded. He then arrived at the correct response.

The video presentation done by her high school ESL students (see Process Writing approach) provided Bryna with the opportunity to assess her students' overall ability to write to a specific audience for a specific purpose. By viewing both the practice and final presentations of the video, she was able to note how various students revised their work in order to make their presentations clearer to their audience. She noted:

(Observations, Day Seven)
Practicing the reports orally for their partners also proved invaluable in establishing a sense of audience. With an attentive audience right in front of them the students began to spontaneously clarify and elaborate on ideas that were not fully developed. Jatinder realized in reading his report aloud that his original ending was unsatisfactory and developed a different ending.

By having her students act out *The Little Red Hen,* Marta was able to assess how well her deaf kindergartners understood the story. After having been read the story in ASL,[18] the children dramatized it.

---

[18]Children look at English text while teacher interprets using ASL.

Throughout the dramatization, Marta was able to observe and note how well Nancy, playing the main character, sequenced the story. She assessed other students' ability to understand the characters in the story as they acted out their parts in the play:

> Nancy has all the appropriate props and proceeds to busy herself with the hen's work trying to follow the sequence set forth in the story. Tommy is playing an excellent dog staying in character by improvising and going to the refrigerator for some imaginary food, he then goes back to sleep. Mike, Sara, and Donnie are having a more difficult time creating spontaneous language about other characters (gossiping). We did model the character for him, but sustaining conversation with Donnie and Sara, whose expressive language is limited, was a difficult task for him. Mike improvised by inviting his guest into the kitchen for food. The surroundings and food props were familiar to Donnie and Sara, and this enabled them to converse in a comfortable setting at their own level.

The Home–School Connection

An often underutilized source for assessing the complete literacy development of bilingual students is information on home literacy activities.[19] Many bilingual students are often the more proficient second-language speakers in the home, and may be the only first language literate members of their family, or they are frequently relied on to read important information sent to the home in the second language, fill out necessary applications and other forms, interpret bills and legal documents, and so forth.

Logs could be kept by either by the students or their parents in which literacy activities are recorded, indicating the languages used, the types of activities, the purpose, and any other pertinent information. These activities should not be prescribed by the teacher, bur rather should be naturally occurring and could include writing journals; reading books or manuals; reading and writing notes to parents/children; reading and writing letters to relatives; reading newspapers and magazines; writing shopping lists; or filling out forms and applications.

CONCLUSION

Getting to know students, creating an atmosphere of respect for their languages and cultures, and conducting fair assessments are vital qualities of literacy instruction. Teachers must address them while implementing the approaches recommended in this handbook.

Learning about students and their beliefs about reading and writing helps personalization of instruction.[20] It also helps maintain high but reasonable ex-

---

[19]Paratore, Homza, Krol-Sinclair, Lewis-Barrow, Melzi, Stergis, and Haynes (1995) describe a home-school literacy project in which parents share students' literacy activities with teachers through a home portfolio.

[20]See Sizer (1992) for the importance of considering students as individuals and the different factors that contribute to the differences among students.

pectations of students. Teachers working with students in their second language should be particularly careful not to reach conclusions about their students based on their classroom behavior. Some students cope well and quickly flourish and others do not. Unusual performance and behavior, caused by language and culture shock, may lead to incorrect perceptions of their personalities and cognitive abilities. Teachers should ask parents and other teachers about students with difficulties and observe students while they function in their native language in order to form a more accurate representation of such students.

A bilingual–bicultural approach to teaching creates a classroom atmosphere that accepts all languages and cultures as rich vehicles for learning. In such classrooms, languages and cultures connect teachers with students, enhance their learning, and foster linguistic and academic learning. The knowledge the students bring serves as a foundation to further develop that knowledge and to introduce students to new ideas and perspectives. Helping students keep a balance and insuring accommodation between the cultures is a crucial aspect of educating bilingual learners.

A bilingual–bicultural approach is beneficial not only to bilingual students but to English speakers. Awareness of other languages and special work on English for the sake of students who are learning it as a second language enhances the teaching of English for all students.

Assessment is best carried out as an integral part of teaching. While observing students and trying to understand their strengths and weaknesses, teachers enhance their knowledge about bilingual learners, improve their teaching, and become more fair and accurate in their judgment of students. Moreover, students' performance often depends on the particular task. Teachers can try different tasks if one fails to provide credible information. Assessment that is coordinated with instruction results in better assessment and better instruction.

6

Learning From Students' Performance

"Teachers are seen—and principally see themselves—as consumers rather than producers of knowledge."[1] Yet closely observing students offers natural opportunities to reflect on teaching and learning. By analyzing their experiences in the classroom, good teachers enhance their skills. By further disseminating what they have learned, such teachers can become significant producers of knowledge. Good schools support teacher research[2], provide opportunities for teachers to share their findings with other educators, and incorporate teacher research into the agenda of school improvement.

Relating instruction and assessment, even informally, to research improves classroom practices. By conducting research, teachers (a) systematize teaching and assessment, (b) evaluate their own teaching, (c) relate their practices to other research, (d) use innovative instructional practices other than talking and lecturing, and (e) collaborate and share ideas with colleagues. Extending data collection to documentation of learning in the home enhances communication between teachers and families.

Teachers routinely collect data by observing, making mental notes, formally assessing students, and saving student products. When teachers add careful analysis and reflection to this process, they contribute to the body of knowledge about teaching and learning. Because time is a barrier to conducting research, teachers should limit the scope of the research, turn instruction and assessment into data collection opportunities, and contribute to building a culture in schools that supports research and values teachers' findings. Teachers can limit their questions or goals, the amount of time they dedicate to data collection and reflection, and the number of students involved.

---

[1]Freeman (1998, p. 10).
[2]Teacher research is "systematic and intentional inquiry carried out by teachers" (Cochran-Smith & Lytle, 1993, p. 7).

This chapter describes how to conduct research while implementing literacy practices recommended in this handbook.[3] The process includes:

- Planning and preparation.
- Implementation and data collection.
- Analysis, reflection, and dissemination.

The process is illustrated through a project carried out by a teacher over the period of 12 weeks.

PLANNING AND PREPARATION

In planning research within the context of their teaching and assessment, teacher–researchers follow these steps:

- Describe students
- Assess reading and writing in both languages
- Review approaches and choose one or more
- Set goals for research by concentrating on:
  a) one aspect of students' development
  b) chosen teaching approaches
- Read research about:
  a) specific aspect of student development
  b) chosen approaches
- Evaluate appropriateness of classroom layout
- Design study

Information about the learners, an essential initial step for instruction and assessment, is also the first phase of research. Teachers must gauge students' needs and the particular literacy approaches to decide which approaches to use and in what combination. Students' literacy skills in both native and second languages are assessed through testing, observation, and interviewing other teachers, parents, and the students themselves. Other information collected about the students (see Appendix A) determines strengths, needs, and interests, as well as students' linguistic, educational, and cultural backgrounds.

An overview of the approaches, as well as reading more in depth about those that appear suitable, helps teachers make and justify decisions on the approach or approaches to use. By reviewing relevant research, teachers can understand better why they are following particular steps or procedures. Familiarity with the theoretical foundation of each approach allows for modifying approaches to suit particular students.

---

[3]This research can be done individually by a teacher or as part of the work required of professional development or university courses.

Next, questions are formulated or goals are set based on the knowledge of both students and the chosen approaches. Goals or questions relate to specific skills teachers hope their students will develop and to the effectiveness of the approach chosen.

By outlining a study design, teachers collect data while instructing and assessing. Implementation of the literacy approach and assessment can be done for all students in the class and the research component can focus on a few students. Although the whole class is engaged in writing, the teacher might collect data on a small group of students.

An alternative is to do both implementation and research with only a group of students. Katherine, for example, wanted to study higher order thinking skills in students' oral discussions and response journals. She chose ten students with whom she worked during nine 45-minute sessions, videotaping their sessions and collecting their journals. The rest of her students completed assignments supervised by a classroom paraprofessional. The experience taught her how to better facilitate the process of reading comprehension and how to encourage thinking skills. After the study, she then used these approaches with her whole class. The students who had participated in the small group project assisted the rest of the class making elaborations, inferences, and syntheses of their readings.

Steps in a research design include initial assessment of students, data collection, analysis, and reflection. For example, a teacher choosing the Reader-Generated Questions approach with the goal of developing ability to make predictions might follow closely students reading four selections over a period of four weeks. Each week a different group would be studied. After introducing the reading selection, students in each group write questions they think the selection will answer and guess answers for their questions. Students then read the passage, check their responses, and write summaries. The teacher observes and takes notes on the focus group of the week. The students' ability to predict independently, with help from classmates, or not at all, is gleaned from sheets with students' questions and answers and from teacher's notes. The teacher assesses the summaries for the main idea and number of details to obtain data on reading comprehension. These results are not only used for the research project, but become part of the assessment records of the students. As with all research, original plans may need modification once instruction takes place.

Teachers analyze the setting to determine if it facilitates the implementation of the particular approach. For example, Reader-Generated Questions requires whole class, group, and individual work arrangements.

IMPLEMENTATION AND DATA COLLECTION

Teachers try the chosen approach with their class in the context of their regular instructional and assessment agenda. Teachers implement the chosen approach and gather data following the plan in their study design. The following activities occur simultaneously:

- Implementation of the approach
- Collection of data
- Sharing with colleagues (and course instructor if done as part of professional development)

There are a number of ways to collect data while teaching. Teachers can write notes on copies of students' products to detail students' performance around these products. In personal files, teachers keep classroom observations, self-memoranda, and audio and video recordings. Classroom observations include factual descriptions and verbatim quotes. Any thoughts that come to mind should be noted by clearly marking with parenthesis or by adding o.c. (occasional comment) to distinguish from the facts. For example, as Laura was observing her students during Dialogue Journal she notes:

> Eduardo brought stickers to personalize his journal [o.c.: this indicates to me that he is interested in his piece].

Teachers write such notes while the students pursue group or individual work. Some teachers use sticky pads or address labels to write quick reminder notes or a student quote. They can write memoranda at the end of the day. These should be free-flowing descriptions of facts, ideas, reflections, or a synthesis of events over time. Using chart paper, rather than a board, they compile and save ideas produced by the whole class. Audio tape or video recordings are very helpful in collecting accurate information.[4] Any formal or informal assessment becomes part of the data sources.

Teachers organize their data in students' portfolios and personal files. Teachers create a portfolio for each focus student. The portfolio includes the protocol with general information about the student (Appendix A) , instructional goals, assessment results, and student products. Such data collected for the purpose of research are useful for evaluating students' performance. It is a natural extension of student assessment, allowing for assessment not only of products but of process.

The systematic collection of samples of students' performance required for research purposes provides authentic data on students' abilities over time and without the distortions of stress typical of test situations. As shown in the section on assessment, Laurie's observations of Teddy's performance (see chap. 5) while reading provided a clear picture of his reading difficulties and his improvement over time.

---

[4]See Freeman (1998, Appendix C), for detailed suggestions on data collection strategies.

The length of time dedicated to data collection depends on the frequency and nature of the project and goals. Five weeks of daily observations may provide adequate data as can bi-weekly collection over 6 to 10 weeks. Carrying the approach through a full cycle is essential to answer questions about the approach.

ANALYSIS, REFLECTION, AND DISSEMINATION

Much learning occurs in this last phase where teachers:

- Analyze results.
- Discuss results with colleagues.
- Draw conclusions and relate to existing research.
- Make recommendations.
- Disseminate their findings.

Teachers analyze and reflect on data collected, at times leading to changes while implementing the approach. They also analyze their data collected over a few weeks chronologically, thematically, or both. They either focus on all students together or on individual students. Much depends on the particular nature of the project and the variability on student performance. This analysis encourages teachers to reflect on their students' performance over time. It gives teachers a clearer picture of their students' development than impressions formed from one day to the next. It also illustrates the impact of a particular approach on students. Often teachers are surprised at how much students have developed and how different ways of implementing the various stages of the approach helped or hindered the process. For example, going back to our example of developing and studying the ability to predict doing the Reader-Generated Questions approach, the teacher analyzes each student's questions to see if the questions are connected to the topic of the reading. The teacher also reviews classroom notes on group discussions for evidence of improved performance with the help of classmates. These notes can shed light on students' interpretation of the topic, misunderstandings, and cultural differences.

Careful analysis of data reveals goals attained, questions answered, or even unexpected findings about the literacy approaches and their students' development. Teachers arrive at a concrete realization of their students' learning and their own teaching through reflection on the results, comparison with other studies, and discussions with colleagues. They also decide which approaches merit implementation and how best to modify them. This process enlightens teachers as to the way bilingual students function.

Collaboration is essential for this type of research. All projects described in this handbook were carried out within literacy courses offered either on campus or at the school districts. Course participants worked in groups discussing and critiquing each other's plans, goals, assessment strategies, implementation, data collection, and analysis. Such experiences might be replicated in teacher-led study groups.[5]

Disseminating findings is valuable both to teacher-researchers and their colleagues. A poster session is a good initial way to disseminate findings. Teachers present, in a clear and didactic fashion, the key results and conclusions of their research on a poster board. Four or five participants present simultaneously in their own stations while the audience walks around looking at their posters and asking questions. This format is less threatening than a conference presentation and provides a rehearsal for presentations at conferences or school workshops.

Teachers can use these research strategies to try new approaches not included in this volume. Through this systematic observation of students' performance, they can evaluate the effectiveness of any approach, what aspects of literacy the approach helps develop, how the students react, and what modifications can be introduced to improve bilingual learning.

A TEACHER-RESEARCHER IN ACTION[6]

Ivelisse, a middle school bilingual teacher, works in a bilingual special education resource room where some students stay all day and others come for special help. She received a tuition voucher to attend a graduate course in literacy. She carried out her research as a class project, sharing her work throughout the semester with the course instructor and classmates.

After reading about various approaches described in chapters 2, 3, and 4, class participants discussed the approaches and their students in order to find the best match. Ivelisse described her students' reading comprehension difficulties. She was particularly interested in María, a 14-year-old Puerto Rican student with a history of language and literacy difficulties. She decided to look into the use of Graphic Organizers.

For the first four weeks Ivelisse gathered information on María using the protocol provided to class participants as a guide (see Appendix A). Conversations with María, her family, and other teachers provided valuable information on María's background. Observations and testing of María's reading and writing skills in Spanish and English revealed, among other things, that she became easily frustrated when making mistakes and had a low opinion of her academic abilities. She had difficulty with story elements, predictions, and oral retellings in Spanish. She had little knowledge of English. To assess María's reading comprehension, Ivelisse read her a first-grade level book, *Ricitos de Oro y los Tres Ositos* (*Goldilocks and the Three Bears*). Her comprehension of the story was extremely limited and confused. Of eight comprehension questions

---

[5]See Clair (1998) for research on teacher study groups.
[6]Ivelisse Nelson carried out this project.

Ivelisse asked, María could only answer two accurately. She shrugged her shoulders or answered "I don't know" to four. The other two were completely or partially incorrect.

Ivelisse had some experience using story maps as a postreading activity. She decided to use Graphic Organizers as a prereading as well as postreading activity after becoming familiar with the variety of uses of this approach and concluding that they would be especially useful to María as a concrete learner. Spanish, María's dominant language, was chosen as the language of instruction. Ivelisse set as a goal for the project the improvement of María's reading comprehension of first-grade level Spanish books. She wanted to investigate if using Graphic Organizers would assist María in identifying accurately the various story elements.

The classroom where Ivelisse worked had several tables appropriate for group work. They had resources in English and Spanish as well as computer facilities and access to the Internet. Ivelisse worked with the focus group at one of the tables while the other resource teacher taught students at a separate table. The conditions of the room were well suited for the implementation of the project.

Implementation and Data Collection

Ivelisse used Graphic Organizers with a small group of students everyday for 5 weeks during her 55-minute literacy period. The first story was *Coco Ya No Espera Más* about a girl and her grandmother who kept missing each other when visiting. Ivelisse introduced the theme with the poem *Abuelita* (*Grandmother*) by Tomás Allende Iragorri. Students then created a variety of semantic maps (as a group and individually) with ideas on what they liked to do with their grandmothers, how they travel to visit their grandmothers, and their family tree. These maps provided a good opportunity to develop vocabulary. Students drew a picture illustrating a visit to their own grandmother.

Ivelisse then showed the cover of the book and wrote predictions from students about the content of the story. Ivelisse read the story aloud, given her students' difficulty reading. She frequently stopped to discuss what was happening, to discuss illustrations, and to make further predictions. After reading, they reviewed the prediction chart. Then students individually filled in story elements in individual story charts and illustrated a sequence map, annotating their drawings. For the final activity, students received a sheet with a square and lines below where they were to draw and write about their favorite story part.

Ivelisse kept notes on what happened during her lessons with special emphasis on what María was doing. She wrote:

> I invited my students to share something about their grandmother and to say what
> kind of things they like to do with her. María started hugging herself, while an-
> swering "gusta cuando me acaricia"(I like being hugged), "gusta hablar" (I like

to talk to her), "ir a la tienda" (go to the store). María continued to answer, while I wrote on the board. After giving several answers she copied from the board what she likes to do with her grandmother on a personal web. [o.c. It seems easier for María to read what she copies on her own paper] (Ivelisse's field notes 2/9/98).

Ivelisse typed her daily observations, filing them on her classroom computer. She also created a portfolio with copies of María's various individual semantic maps and story drawings. Ivelisse brought copies of her observations and students' products every week to her class at the university. Working in pairs, course participants exchanged observations, read them, and then asked each other questions for clarification. Special emphasis was placed on objective and descriptive information.[7] For example, Ivelisse had written: " ... students were asked to draw themselves visiting one of their grandmothers. María seemed confused ... " (Ivelisse's field notes, 2/12/98). Cristina, Ivelisse's colleague, asked her what María had done to appear confused. After checking her handwritten notes, Ivelisse added to her observation:

María's first reaction was "Cómo? Yo no sé" (How? I don't know.).

Ivelisse handed her observations to the course instructor for further reaction to both her teaching and her data collection strategies.

Analysis and Reporting Results

Ivelisse used data in her computer files and portfolio for periodic assessment of and reporting on María's progress as well as for her research project. To analyze data, Ivelisse grouped observations and María's products into three stages: prereading, reading, and postreading activities. For each period she analyzed the strategies used as well as María's performance, looking at everything María said and produced.

Ivelisse analyzed her notes, looking for evidence of what María did and what she said during each of the activities looking for evidence of development. María, helped by this particular approach, began using strategies (prior knowledge and prediction) in the reading process that are characteristic of good readers. Her requests for help were mostly for spelling.

A comparison between María's story map and her initial reading comprehension assessment reveals María's comprehension of stories improved. In her initial assessment, María missed one main character, did not know the setting, the problem, or solution of the test story. She could only report one event correctly. Writing her story map after reading Coco's story, María was able to correctly fill in main characters and most additional characters, setting, problem, and solution. She filled in all the sections of the story map, unlike her initial assessment, where half of the answers were a shrug of the shoulders.

---

[7]Course participants used the guidelines of the approach Show Not Tell (chap. 2) to critique each other's field notes.

Analysis of an earlier and later version of the sequence map shows that María could correctly sequence the story after additional reading. She included most events in her first attempt at a sequence map, although some of the order was not correct. She was able to complete it and sequence it correctly after an additional reading of the story. By using a sequence map, María was able to express her thoughts through drawings and labels. These maps show the student's drawing and writing abilities and corrections she made.

Throughout the process, Ivelisse met during her university class with three other students to discuss María's performance and progress in her research. Much of the discussion took place in Spanish, a language common to all members of that group. The course instructor was often called on to answer questions or provide clarification.

Reflection and Dissemination

In discussing her results, Ivelisse concludes that the instructional approach had helped María achieve the main goal of identifying story parts and improving reading comprehension. María still had some difficulty with characters, spelling, and other aspects of language. Rereading the story after having established some comprehension filled in details.

Graphic Organizers helped prepare students for reading and allowed them to demonstrate understanding a story in concrete and manageable ways using drawings and single words. In María's case, this approach enhanced her classroom participation. After the first couple of sessions, María stopped saying "Yo no sé" (I don't know) or shrugging her shoulders, responses characteristic of this learner in the initial evaluations and observations.

Ivelisse states that she learned the importance of preparing students for reading as a result of this project. The concreteness and style of Graphic Organizers greatly help students who feel overwhelmed when looking at extended text.

At the final meeting of the course, Ivelisse presented a poster consisting of three panels. On the left side she illustrated prereading activities with copies of María's semantic maps and drawings, on the right side were postreading activities such as the story web and sequence map. In the middle Ivelisse stated what the project did for her student and recommendations about the use of Graphic Organizers. Discussion and questions during the poster session drew further reflection and ideas for future implementation.

Careful choice of a reading approach and analysis and reflection of its implementation helped Ivelisse realize that there are ways to improve her students' performance. Writing and sharing her research concretely demonstrated to Ivelisse her capacity for teaching and her students' ability to learn.

CONCLUSION

The need to prepare and retool teachers in literacy instruction for bilingual and second-language learners is great. The numbers of students entering American schools with languages other than English or in addition to English continue to increase. There is also growing interest in expanding second-language education for English speakers. Success for such students requires becoming truly functional in another language.

This handbook presents practical ideas as well as a process for preparing good literacy instructors. There is no question that knowledge of the students' native language facilitates instruction in the second language, especially for beginners. However, the process documented in this handbook has been useful for many teachers who are not bilingual, helping them gain expertise and confidence to teach students in their second language. "I learned a great deal concerning many areas of bilingual education using this approach [Process Writing]" declared a computer teacher working for the first time with bilingual students. She adds, "These students were all strangers to me in September but I feel that I know them well now."

Theory, practice, and research, the three components in the process of teacher preparation (see Fig. 6.1), are important and sustain each other. Teachers must be grounded in the theory of literacy and bilingualism as well as teaching approaches and assessment. This knowledge informs instruction and assessment. Teachers carry out instruction and assessment while they test the value of content knowledge through their research. Their reflections and conclusions enhance theory and practice.

Although the focus of this handbook is to present useful approaches for teaching literacy to bilingual learners, preservice and in-service teachers bene-

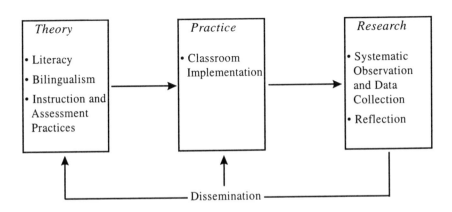

FIG. 6.1. Content and process for preparing literacy teachers.

fit from experiencing the whole process of theory acquisition, practice, and research. By researching the implementation of these approaches, teachers gain a solid grounding on how to work with bilingual and second-language learners. What they learn in many cases greatly differs from their initial notions about bilingualism and second-language learning and how to teach literacy. Teachers acquire lasting knowledge about diverse populations through first-hand experience with these learners coupled with guided reflection and instruction.[8]

---

[8]Coppola (1998) studied teachers using the Critical Autobiographies approach.

Appendix A: Protocol To Gather Information About Learners

The following shows a protocol for gathering information about learners.

NAME:
External and family characteristics
Country or place of origin
Reasons for coming to the U.S. (learner or family)
Date of arrival ——————— Born in the U.S. ———————
Intended length of stay in USA
Parents' occupation
Parents' education
Parents' language and literacy ability
Uses of literacy at home (specify languages)
Family attitudes toward native language and culture
Family attitudes toward English and American culture
Language(s) used at home for speaking
Language(s) used at home for reading/writing
Personal characteristics
- Age
- Oral language proficiency in L1
- Oral language proficiency in L2
- School experience

- Previous school experience (in the home country)
where
how long
language(s) used (specify subject if more than one language used)
student population (majority and minority status)
- Current school experience
how long
language(s) used (specify subject if more than one language used)
student population (majority and minority status)
- Attitudes toward L1 and L2
- Personal goals for L2 and L2 literacy
- Personality traits
- Interests
- Outside of class responsibilities (helping family)
- Is s/he physically challenged?
- Are there issues in regard to substance abuse or mental health?
Characteristics as reader and writer
Language(s) in which literacy was initiated
L1 literacy level (and how it was determined)
L2 literacy level (and how it was determined)
Attitude toward reading and writing
Language preference for reading and writing
Conception of literacy
- Motivation for reading and writing
- Preferred strategies for reading and writing
Other characteristics:

Appendix B:
Additional Approaches

FRAMEWORK FOR CRITICAL LITERACY
(Adapted from Alma Flor Ada, 1988)

This framework includes four phases for the discussion of reading, each increasing the level of creative thinking.

Descriptive phase: the interaction is based on the information contained in the text. The answers for questions asked are contained in the text. For example: where/when/what happened? Who did it? Why?

Personal interpretative phase: students relate the information to their own experience and feelings. Questions such as: Did you ever experience something like this? How did what you read make you feel? Did you like it?

Critical analysis phase: students relate what was learned from the text to broader issues; they draw inferences and make generalizations. Questions such as: Is what the text says valid? Always? Why? Are there alternatives?

Creative action phase: students apply what they learned to real situations.

For example, to apply the framework to fiction: (1) have the students read a story about an immigrant child and discuss what happened, (2) have them discuss how it compares with their lives, (3) then discuss whether it always happens that way, and (4) finally, have them discuss what they can do to solve some of their own problems as immigrants or migrant students of a different language.

To apply the framework to expository text, you could: (1) have the children read about the causes and prevention of fires and discuss what the reading says, (2) discuss any personal experience with fires, (3) discuss and compare various causes and prevention, and (4) make plans to improve the conditions in their own homes, learn fire department's phone number, and so on.

References

Ada, A. F. (1988). The Pájaro Valley experience. In T. Skutnabb-Kangas & J. Cummins (Eds.), *Minority education: From shame to struggle* (pp. 223–238). Clevedon, UK: Multilingual Matters.
Cummins, J. (1994). Knowledge, power, and identity in teaching English as a second language. In F. Genesee (Ed.), *Educating second language children* (pp. 33–58). New York: Cambridge University Press.

K-W-L

To execute the K-W-L approach:

1. Establish the topic for reading or writing.
2. Make three columns on the blackboard.
3. Put the following titles above each column: I know, I want to learn, I learned.

I KNOW	I WANT TO LEARN	I LEARNED

4. Discuss with your students what they know about the topic and list it in the first column.
5. Ask them what they would like to learn and list it under the second column (it can be done in the form of questions).
6. Have the students read a passage in that particular content area.
7. Have them discuss what they learned and list it in the third column.
8. Have them write about it.

References

Ogle, D. (1986). A teaching model that develops active reading of expository text. *The Reading Teacher, 39*, 564–570.

READING ALOUD

Have a reading corner where you can seat comfortably on a round, with the classroom library nearby. It is helpful, when reading aloud, to:

1. Choose a story that you and the children like or let the children choose. It is better if it is a short story from traditional children's literature. You should be able to read it in one sitting.
2. Give students a general sense of what the story is about either by introducing the main character, or talking generally about the story (let them use native language to clarify among themselves). Do not spend too much time at this. If they have read this story before, you may want to skip this step.
3. Read with expression, not too fast, but flowing. Let the children join in, make comments, and ask questions. Eventually they will learn to listen to the whole story. Be patient, and do not discipline them, you want to make it a fun activity.
4. After it is finished, let children make comments on their own. Do not question them.
5. Leave books handy so that children can read on their own these same books.

References

Trelease, J. (1982). *The reading aloud handbook.* New York: Penguin.
Trelease, J. (1989). Jim Trelease speaks on reading aloud to children. *The Reading Teacher, 12,* 200–206.

RHETORICAL APPROACH
(Adapted from de Alvarado, 1984)

To conduct the Rhetorical approach:

1. *Choose and explore the topic.* Choose a general topic or have the class choose a topic. Ask students to write a page on this topic (anything they want). Tell them it will not be seen or corrected. Let them discuss in groups what they each wrote about.
2. *Define the purpose and audience.* Have them discuss and list possible reasons for writing about the topic and the different kinds of audiences they would write about. Have them choose one of the situations and audiences. (Either the whole class chooses one, or each group chooses one.)
3. *Narrow the topic.* Have them discuss and list subtopics from general to particular given the decision made in Step 2.
4. *Consider genre and organization.* Have them discuss and decide on the genre and organization, considering the content, audience, and genre they have in mind.
5. *Select information.* Decide specific information that will be included.

6. *Write the draft.* Based on Steps 3, 4, and 5, write drafts individually. (This can be done in class and as homework.) The teacher can be available for any questions. Have bilingual dictionaries and grammars available.

7. *Edit.* Groups form again to help edit each other's work. The teacher can prepare some questions for the students or he or she can do it with each group to show them how to look at a draft. Clarity of content and organization should be the first order of priority, then comes vocabulary, grammar, punctuation, and spelling.

8. *Produce the final copy.* Each group is responsible for working on a final copy. Let students edit as much as they want, initially. And let them decide when they are ready to prepare the final copy. When something is chosen for publishing, then it has to be completely edited without any mistakes.

9. *Publish students' writing.* The teacher should look for opportunities for publishing students' writing. Opportunities can include the school newspaper or a magazine, a district newsletter, or a local paper or contest.

References

Carson, J. F., & Leki, I. (Eds.). (1993). *Reading in the composition classroom.* Boston, MA: Heinle & Heinle.

de Alvarado, C. S. (1984). From topic to final paper: A rhetorical approach. *TESOL Newsletter, 2,* 9–10.

Johnson, D. M., & Roen, D. H. (Eds.). (1989). *Richness in writing: Empowering ESL students.* New York: Longman.

Appendix C:
Graphic Organizers

Sense Matrix

Looks like	Smells like	Sounds like	Feels like	Tastes like

Story Map for Primary Grades

TITLE/AUTHOR
SETTING
MAIN CHARACTERS
BEGINNING OF STORY
MIDDLE OF STORY
END OF STORY

Story Map For Intermediate Students

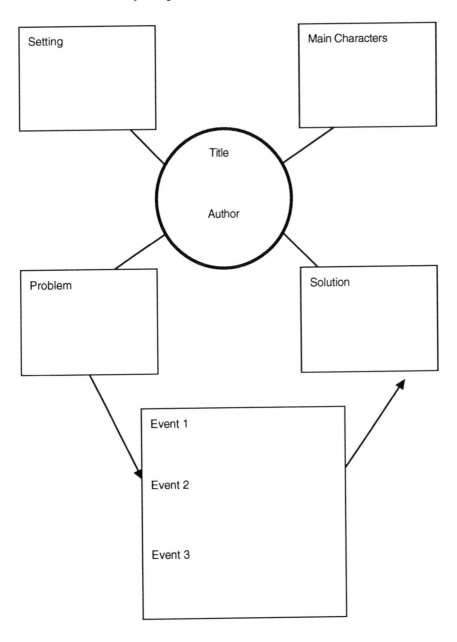

Setting

Main Characters

Title

Author

Problem

Solution

Event 1

Event 2

Event 3

Summary of Expository Text

MAIN TOPIC

SUB-TOPIC 1	SUB-TOPIC 2	SUB-TOPIC 3
Main Idea	Main Idea	Main Idea
Details	Details	Details

VENN DIAGRAM

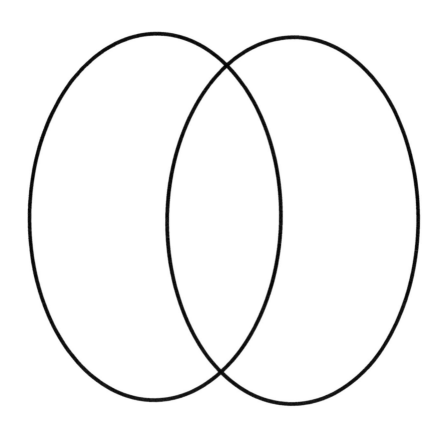

Appendix D:
Assessment Practices

The following is a brief explanation of some of the recommended assessment practices:

- *Oral Interviews*: Students are asked in a conversational manner to explain what they have learned, understood, or interpreted from a text or lesson. It can also be used to have students explain why they wrote something in a certain way.
- *Read Alouds*: Students read passages from text through which teachers can evaluate fluency and word attack skills.
- *Retellings*: Students recall in descriptive detail and sequentially all the important events of a story. Through retellings, teachers can assess vocabulary development, sequencing of a story, identification of main idea, details, characters, setting, plot, and so forth.
- *Writing Samples*: Students submit different samples (original stories, poems, songs, expository essays) of their own written work in various stages of the writing process (i.e., graphic organizers, first draft, revised sample, edited sample, final drafts, etc.). Teachers can then determine what is to be assessed, for example, organization of content, beginning, middle, end of story, use of descriptive words, character development, use of invented spelling, use of conventional spelling, standard grammar usage, correct use of punctuation, knowledge of audience, clear purpose for writing, revisions, and editing.
- *Experiments/Demonstrations*: Students show knowledge and understanding of what has been read by performing an experiment or showing, through active demonstration, that a concept has been mastered. Teachers can assess for completeness of thought, understanding of main idea, attention to details, and vocabulary development.

- *Projects/Exhibitions*: Through projects and exhibitions students are able to demonstrate, in a multidimensional manner, knowledge, understanding, and application of a concept or lesson. This type of evaluation is especially helpful for the emerging literate student, as well as the second-language student, because it does not rely exclusively on written language.
- *Response Journals*: After the reading of a book, or a passage from a book, students write their reactions in a journal. Teacher-initiated prompts eliciting responses to character development, plot details, vocabulary use, author's purpose, or student's personal reaction to the text can be done. Students may also write freely in response to the reading or a discussion.
- *Learning Logs*: Learning logs can be used to evaluate students' understanding of a concept learned. Students write what they have learned about a specific topic or lesson. Teachers can use learning logs to assess what was actually understood by the students, and what aspects of a lesson may need to be reviewed or retaught.
- *Constructed Responses*: Open-ended questions about a lesson or a passage read are given to assess comprehension. Teachers can assess specific concept understanding of content area passages by using constructed responses.
- *Conferences*: Much can be learned and assessed through individual conferences with students. Conferences can be used to evaluate a student's understanding of a text, or strategies a student uses when faced with unknown words or concepts.

References

Ashton-Warner, S. (1963). *Teacher.* New York: Simon & Schuster.

August, D., & Hakuta, K. (Eds.). (1997). *Improving schooling for language-minority children.* Washington, DC: National Academy Press.

Basham, C. S., & Kwachka, P. E. (1991). Reading the world differently: A cross-cultural approach to writing assessment. In L. Hamp-Lyons (Ed.), *Assessing second-lang- uage writing in academic contexts* (pp. 37–49). Norwood, NJ: Ablex.

Benesch, S. (1993). Reading and writing critical autobiographies. In J. G. Carson & I. Leki (Eds.), *Reading in the composition classroom* (pp. 247–257). Boston, MA: Heinle & Heinle.

Boone, R. (Ed.). (1991). *Teaching process writing with computers.* Eugene, OR: International Society for Technology in Education.

Brisk, M. E. (1985). Using the computer to develop literacy among bilingual students. *Equity and Choice, 1* (7), 25–32.

Brisk, M. E. (1998a). *Bilingual education: From compensatory to quality schooling.* Mahwah, NJ: Lawrence Erlbaum Associates.

Brisk, M. E. (1998b). *The transforming power of critical autobiographies.* Boston, MA: Boston College. (ERIC Document Reproduction Service No. ED 424739).

Brisk, M. E., & Zandman, D. (1995). A journey through immigration: Writing a critical autobiography. *Chelkat Lashon, 19–20,* 87–117.

Buckley, M. H., & Boyle, O. F. (1981). *Mapping the writing journey.* Berkeley: University of California/Bay Area Writing Project.

Caplan, R. (1983). Showing, not telling. In M. Myers & J. Grey (Eds.), *Theory and practice in the teaching of composition* (pp. 226–238). Chicago, IL: National Council of Teachers of English.

Clair, N. (1998). Teacher study groups: Persistent questions in a promising approach. *TESOL Quarterly, 32,* 465–492.

Cochran-Smith, M., & Lytle, S. (1993). *Inside/outside: Teacher research and knowledge.* New York: Teacher's College.

Conklin, N. F., & Lourie, M. A. (1983). *A host of tongues: Language communities in the United States.* New York: The Free Press.

Connor, U., & Kaplan, R. B. (Eds.). (1987). *Writing across languages: Analysis of L2 text.* Reading, MA: Addison-Wesley.

Coppola, J. (1998). *Teachers learning about diversity: Effects on curricular and instructional decisions in literacy.* Unpublished doctoral dissertation, Boston University.

Cummins, J. (1991). Interdependence of first- and second-language proficiency in bilingual children. In E. Bialystok (Ed.), *Language processing in bilingual children* (pp. 70–89). New York: Cambridge University Press.

Cummins, J., & Sayers, D. (1995). *Brave new schools: Challenging cultural illiteracy.* New York: St. Martin's Press.

Daiute, C. (1985). *Writing and computers.* Reading, MA: Addison-Wesley

D'Angelo Bromley, K. (1989). Buddy journals make the reading-writing connection. *The Reading Teacher, 43,* 122–129.

Dixon, C., & Nessel, D. (1983). *Language experience approach to reading and writing.* New York: Alemany Press.

Donoahue, Z., Van Tassell, M.A., & Patterson, L. (1996). *Research in the classroom: Talk, texts, and inquiry.* Newark, NJ: International Reading Association.

Duranti, A., & Ochs, E. (1995). *Syncretic literacy: Multiculturalism in Samoan American families.* Santa Cruz, CA: The National Center for Research on Cultural Diversity and Second Language Learning.

Edelsky, C. (1989). Bilingual children's writing: Fact or fiction. In D. M. Johnson & D. H. Roen (Eds.), *Richness in writing: Empowering ESL students* (pp. 165–176). New York: Longman.

Faltis, C. J., & Hudelson, S. J. (1998). *Bilingual education in elementary and secondary school communities.* Boston: Allyn & Bacon.

Farr, B. P., & Trumbull, E. (1997). *Assessment alternatives for diverse classrooms.* Norwood, MA: Christopher-Gordon.

Flood, J., & Lapp, D. (1988). Mapping for understanding information texts. *The Reading Teacher, (April),* 780–783.

Forcier, R. C. (1996). *The computer as a productivity tool in education.* Englewood Cliffs, NJ: Merrill.

Freeman, D. (1998). *Doing teacher research: From inquiry to understanding.* Boston: Heinle & Heinle.

Freeman, Y. S., & Freeman, D. E. (1989). Whole language approaches to writing with secondary students of English as a second language. In D. M. Johnson & D. H. Roen (Eds.), *Richness in writing: Empowering ESL students* (pp. 177–192). New York: Longman.

Freeman, Y. S., & Freeman, D. E. (1998). *ESL/EFL teaching: Principles for success.* Portsmouth, NH: Heinemann.

Gee, J. P. (1989). What is literacy? *Journal of Education, 171,* 18–25.

Gee, J. P. (1992). *The social mind: Language, ideology, and social practice.* New York: Bergin & Garvey.

Genesee, F., & Hamayan, E. V. (1994). Classroom-based assessment. In F. Genesee (Ed.), *Educating second language children* (pp. 212–239). Cambridge, England: Cambridge University Press.

Gillespie, C. (1990). Questions about student-generated questions. *Journal of Reading, 34,* 250–257.

Goldenberg, C., Reese, L., & Gallimore, R. (1995). Effects of literacy materials from school on Latino children's home experiences and early reading achievement. In G. Gonzalez & L. Maez (Eds.), *Compendium of research on bilingual education* (pp. 135–157). Washington, DC: National Clearinghouse for Bilingual Education.

Graves, D. H. (1983). *Writing: Teachers & children at work*. Portsmouth, NH: Heinemann Educational Books.

Grosjean, F. (1982). *Life with two languages*. Cambridge, MA: Harvard University Press.

Grosjean, F. (1989). Neurolinguists, beware! The bilingual is not two monolinguals in one person. *Brain and Language, 36*, 3–15.

Hakuta, K., & D'Andrea, D. (1992). Some properties of bilingual maintenance and loss in Mexican background high-school students. *Applied Linguistics, 13*, 72–99.

Heath, S. B. (1983). *Way with words: Language, life and work in communities and classrooms*. Cambridge, England: Cambridge University Press.

Heath, S. B. (1986). Sociocultural contexts of language development. In California Association for Bilingual Education, *Beyond language: social and cultural factors in schooling language minority students* (pp. 143–186). Los Angeles: Evaluation, Dissemination and Assessment center.

Henry, R. (1984). Reader-generated questions: A tool for improving reading comprehension. *TESOL Newsletter (June)*, 4–5.

Holdaway, D. (1984). Developmental teaching of literacy. In D. Holdaway, (Ed.), *Stability and change in literacy learning* (pp. 33–47). Exeter, NH: Heinemann.

Homza, A. (1996). Using graphic organizers to develop bilingual literacy processes. *NABE News, 15 (December)*, 15–20.

Hudelson, S. (1984). "Kan yu ret an rayt en ingles": Children become literate in English as a second language. *TESOL Quarterly, 18*, 221–238.

Hulstijn, J. H., & Matter, J. F. (Eds.). (1991). Reading in two languages. *AILA Review, 8*, Amsterdam: Free University Press.

Isom, D. M. (1995). Telecommunications at Paul Robeson High School: Making global connections from the inner city. *Language Association Bulletin, 46* (4), 7, 23.

Jimenez, R. T., García, G. E., & Pearson, P. D. (1995). Three children, two languages, and strategic reading: Case studies in bilingual/monolingual reading. *American Educational Research Journal, 32*, 67–97.

Juel, C. (1991). Cross-age tutoring between student athletes and at-risk children. *The Reading Teacher, 45*, 178–186.

Kagan, S. (1992). *Cooperative learning*. San Juan Capistrano, CA: Resources for Teachers, Inc.

Kreeft Peyton, J. (1990). Dialogue journal writing: Effective student–teacher communication. In A. M. Padilla, H. H. Fairchild, & C. M. Valadez (Eds), *Bilingual education, issues and strategies* (pp. 184–194). Newbury Park, CA: Sage.

Labbo, L. D., & Teale, W. H. (1990). Cross-age reading: A strategy for helping poor readers. *The Reading Teacher, 43*, 362–369.

Lehr, F. (1995). Revision in the writing process. *ERIC Digest*.

Leong, C. K. (1978). Learning to read in English and Chinese: Some psycholinguistic and cognitive considerations. In D. Feitelson (Ed.), *Cross-cultural perspectives on reading and reading research* (pp. 157–173). Newark, DE: International Reading Association.

Lucas, T., & Katz, A. (1994). Reframing the debate: The roles of native languages in English-only programs for language minority students. *TESOL Quarterly, 28*, 537–561.

Lyon, J. (1996). *Becoming bilingual: Language acquisition in a bilingual community*. Clevedon, England: Multilingual Matters.

Mackey, W. (1968). The description of bilingualism. In J. A. Fishman (Ed.), *Readings in the sociology of language* (pp. 554–584). The Hague: Mouton.

Marzano, R. J., Pickering, D., & McTighe, J. (1993). *Assessing student outcomes*. Aurora, CO: McRel Institute.

McCarty, T. L., & Watahomigie, L. J. (1998). Language and literacy in American Indian and Alaska Native communities. In B. Pérez (Ed.), *Sociocultural contexts of language and literacy* (pp. 69–98). Mahwah, NJ : Lawrence Erlbaum Associates.

McLaughlin, B. (1984). *Second language acquisition in childhood, Vol. 1 & 2.* Hillsdale, NJ: Lawrence Erlbaum Associates.

Michaels, S., & Foster, M. (1985). Peer-peer learning: Evidence from a student-run sharing time. In A. Jagger & M. T. Smith-Burke (Eds.), *Observing the language learner* (pp. 143–158). Delaware: International Reading Association.

Myers, E. (1983). Drawing as prewriting in preschool. In M. Myers & J. Grey (Eds.), *Theory and practice in the teaching of composition* (pp. 75–85). Urbana, IL: National Council of Teachers of English.

Myers, M. (1985). *The teacher-researcher: How to study writing in the classroom*. Urbana, IL: National Council of Teachers of English.

O'Malley, J. M., & Valdez Pierce, L. (1996). *Authentic assessment for English language learners: Practical approaches for the K-12 classroom*. Reading, MA: Addison-Wesley.

Paratore, J. R., Homza, A., Krol-Sinclair, B., Lewis-Barrow, T., Melzi, G., Stergis, R., & Haynes, H. (1995). Shifting boundaries in home and school responsibilities: The construction of home-based literacy portfolios by immigrant parents and their children. *Research in the Teaching of English, 29* , 367–389.

Pardon, D. J. (1992). *Jigsawing with wordless picture books*. Paper presented at the annual meeting of the West Regional Conferences of the International Reading Association, Portland, OR. (ERIC Document: ED346433).

Paul, P. V. (1998). *Literacy and deafness: The development of reading, writing, and literate thought*. Boston: Allyn & Bacon.

Peregoy, S. F., & Boyle, O. F. (1996). *Reading, writing and learning in ESL: A resource book for K-12 teachers*. New York: Longman.

Pérez, B. (Ed.). (1998). *Sociocultural contexts of language and literacy*. Mahwah, NJ: Lawrence Erlbaum Associates.

Perez, B., & Torres-Guzman, M. E. (1996). *Learning in two worlds: An integrated Spanish/English biliteracy approach*. (2nd ed.). New York: Longman.

Peterson, R., & Eeds, M. (1990). *Grand conversations: Literature groups in action*. New York: Scholastic.

Prinz, P. (1998). *The influence of strategic teaching on reading in a second language*. Unpublished doctoral dissertation, Boston University.

Radencich, M., & McKay, L. J. (Eds.). (1995). *Flexible groupings for literacy in the elementary grades*. Needham, MA: Allyn & Bacon.

Reyes, M. L. (1991). A process approach to literacy using dialogue journals and literature logs with second language learners. *Research in the Teaching of English, 25*, 291–313.

Rigg, P. (1989). Language experience approach: Reading naturally. In P. Rigg & V. G. Allen (Eds.), *When they don't all speak English: Integrating the ESL students into the regular classroom* (pp. 65–76). Urbana, IL: National Council of Teachers of English.

Romaine, S. (1995). *Bilingualism* (2nd ed.). Cambridge, MA: Blackwell.

Saravia-Shore, M., & Arvizu, S. (Eds.). (1992). *Cross-cultural literacy: Ethnographies of communication in multiethnic classrooms* . New York: Garland.

Savignon, S. (1983). *Communicative competence: Theory and classroom practice.* Reading, MA: Addison-Wesley.

Saville-Troike, M. (1984). What really matters in second language learning for academic achievement? *TESOL Quarterly, 18,* 199–219.

Sizer, T. R. (1992). *Horace's school: Redesigning the American high school.* Boston: Houghton Mifflin.

Snow, C. E., Burns, M. S., & Griffin, P. (1998). *Preventing reading difficulties in young children.* Washington DC: National Academy Press.

Staton, J. (1988). *Dialogue journal communication: Classroom, linguistic, social, and cognitive views.* Norwood, NJ: Ablex.

Stefanakis, E. H. (1998). *Whose judgment counts? Assessing bilingual children, K-3.* Portsmouth, NH: Heinemann.

Torres-Guzman, M. E. (1992). Stories of hope in the midst of despair: Culturally responsive education for Latino students in an alternative high school in New York City. In M. Saravia-Shore & S. Arvizu (Eds.), *Cross-cultural literacy: Ethnographies of communication in multiethnic classrooms* (pp. 477–490). New York: Garland.

Urzua, C. (1995). *Cross-age tutoring.* ERIC Digest.

Wallerstein, N. (1983). *Language and culture in conflict.* Reading, MA: Addison-Wesley.

Wixon, V., & Wixon, P. (1983). Using talk–write in the classroom. In M. Myers & J. Gray (Eds.), *Theory and practice in the teaching of composition: Processing, distancing and modeling* (pp. 129–135). Urbana, IL: National Council of Teachers of English.

Zamel, V. (1985). Responding to student writing. *TESOL Quarterly, 19,* 195–202.

Zoellner, R. (1983). Talk–write: A behavioral pedagogy for composition. In M. Myers & J. Gray (Eds.), *Theory and practice in the teaching of composition: Processing, distancing and modeling* (pp. 122–128). Urbana, IL: National Council of Teachers of English.

Student Book References

Aardema, V. (1975). *Why mosquitoes buzz in people's ears: A West African tale.* New York: Penguin.

Aardema, V. (1979). *Who's in rabbit's house?* New York: Penguin.

Ada, A. F. (1997). *Querido Pedrín.* New York: First Aladdin Paperbacks/Libros Colibrí.

Ahlberg, J., & Ahlberg, A. (1986). *The jolly postman: Or other people's letters.* London: Little.

Anderson, H. C. (1990). *The ugly duckling.* New York: Putnam.

Bang, M. (1987). *Paper crane.* New York: Morrow.

Bantock, N. (1991). *Griffin & Sabine: An extraordinary correspondence.* San Francisco: Chronicle.

Blocksma, M. (1992). *All my toys are on the floor.* Danbury, CT: Grolier Inc.

Carrillo, G. (1982). *The legend of food mountain.* Emeryville, CA: Children's Bk. Pr.

De Paola, T. (1991). *The legend of the Indian paintbrush.* New York: Putnam.

Dooley, N. (1991). *Everybody cooks rice.* Minneapolis, MN: Carolrhoda.

Dorris, M. (1989). *Guests.* New York: Hyperion.

Gantos, J. (1988). *Rotten Ralph's trick or treat.* Boston, MA: Houghton Mifflin.

Gomi, T. (1984). *Coco can't wait.* New York: William Morrow. (Spanish version *Coco ya no espera más,* translated by Aída E. Marcuse.)

Grifalconi, A. (1986). *The village of the round & square houses.* New York: Little, Brown.

Hayes, J. (NA). *The weeping woman/La llorona, a Hispanic legend told in Spanish and English.* El Paso, TX: Cinco Punto Press.

Hinton, S. E. (1968). *The Outsiders.* New York: Bantam.

Jaffe, N. (1993). *Sing, little sack! ¡Canta, saquito! A folktale from Puerto Rico.* New York: Bantam.

Jin, S. (1990). *My first American friend.* Austin, TX: Raintree Steck-Vaughn.

Joslin, S. (1962). *Dear dragon ... and other useful letter forms for young ladies and gentlemen engaged in everyday correspondence.* New York: Harcourt Brace.

Kraus, R. (1987). *Milton the early riser.* Old Tappan, NJ: Simon & Schuster Children's.

Lobel, A. (1979). *Frog and toad are friends.* New York: Harper & Row.

Marshall, E. (1994). *Three by the sea.* New York: Penguin.

McCloskey, R. (1976). *Make way for ducklings.* New York: Penguin.

McKissack, P., & McKissack, I. (1985). *The little red hen.* Chicago: Children's Press.

157

Rylant, C. (1982). *When I was young in the mountains*. New York: Penguin.

San Souci, R. D. (1987). *The legend of scarface*. New York: Bantam.

Sendak, M. (1986). *Chicken soup with rice*. New York: Scholastic Inc.

Silverstein, S. (1987). *The giving tree*. New York: Harper & Row.

Steptoe, J. (1987). *Mufaro's beautiful daughters: An African tale*. New York: William Morrow & Co., Inc.

Torres, B. L. (1990). *The luminous pearl*. New York: Orchard Books.

Williams, T. (1987). *The glass menagerie*. New York: New American Library.

Williamson, T. (1991). *Ricitos de oro y los tres ositos*. Santiago de Chile: Editorial Andrés Bello.

Author Index

Subject Index